LIKE MINISTERING TO LIKE

According to the gift that each has received,
administer it to one another
as good stewards of the manifold grace of God.
(1 Peter 4:10)

Philip E Leonard

Like Ministering to Like

THE ORIGINS AND GROWTH OF
ACCORD,
THE MARRIAGE COUNSELLING SERVICE
IN THE CATHOLIC CHURCH IN IRELAND
A HISTORY

the columba press

First published in 1999 by
the columba press
55a Spruce Avenue, Stillorgan Industrial Park,
Blackrock, Co Dublin

Cover by Bill Bolger
Origination by The Columba Press
Printed in Ireland by Colour Books Ltd, Dublin

ISBN 1 85607 258 4

Acknowledgements
I have drawn extensively from Professor John Marshall's *Fifty Years of Marriage Care*, a definitive history of the English CMAC, (now Marriage Care Ltd). I am indebted to Professor Marshall and to Marriage Care Ltd for permission to quote from this publication for which I have used a special reference throughout, e.g. (M10) = Marshall, page 10.

The author and publisher gratefully acknowledge the permission of the following to use material in their copyright: Geoffrey Chapman for extracts from *Jack Dominian: Lay Prophet?* by J. Dalrymple, 1995; Darton Longman & Todd for extracts from *God Where Are You?* by Gerard Hughes, 1997; Constable & Co Ltd for extracts from *Client Centred Therapy* by Carl R Rogers, 1951; Professor John Marshall and Marriage Care Ltd for 'The Irish Connection' from *Fifty Years of Marriage Care*, 1996; Brooks/Cole Publishing Co for extracts from *The Skilled Helper* by Gerard Egan, 4th Ed, 1990; Nick Tyndall for his amiable 'Reflections on the CMAC'.

Contents

Biographical Notes

Acknowledgements

To my two collaborators on the editorial team, Mary McFadden and Peter Nugent, for their constant support, and also in this context Bernard Cawley, my talented anchor man in England, so generous with his ability and his time.To Darach Connolly and my sons Colum and Niall for their professional advice on the manuscript and to Bishop Walsh, Liz Early, Fr Dan Cavanagh and Fr John Hannan for their support and guidance.

For special help in providing documents, giving interviews or editing script: Brian Howlett, Mary McKeogh, the late Canon O'Leary, Professor John Marshall, Dr Jack Dominian, Fionnuala Arthur, Dr Jim Barnes, John Kernan, Leo O'Donnell, Jim Hewison, Gavin Halpin, Sheila Campbell, Mary Goss, George Steer, Fr Andy Kennedy, Fr Martin Tierney, Dr Raymond Magill, Dr Esther Bradley, Mary Higgins, Dorothy Scally, Veronica Graham-Green and her mother the late Eirene Graham-Green, Monsignor Denis O'Callaghan. To Niall Leonard for researching documents in London and to David McDonald of GCAS in Belfast for transferring photographs to discs.

For their endless help and co-operation: Maureen Warren and the office staff in Dublin, Jennifer Watts in the Belfast office and Helen Davis in London.

Others who willingly helped: John Chambers, Chief Executive of *Relate* in Belfast, Joan Dunlop and *Relate* staff, Eilis Connolly and her brother Fr Brendan McDonnell, the late Cormac O'Connor, Colm O'Doherty, Claire D'Arcy, Joe Mc Fadden, Eithne Maguire, Dr Colm Kelly, Seamus O'Hara, Anne Howard, Ann Small, Moira Gaston, Matt Nolan, Liam Hogan, Michael and Terri Quinn, Patrick Seccombe, Marie Kennedy, Quentin de la Bedoyere, Mary Corbett, Mary Eyre, Bishops F G Brooks, William Walsh and Colm O'Reilly, Tony Campbell, Jim

Meehan, David C Sheehy, Dublin Diocesan Archives, Liam Murphy, John McLaughlin, Seamus Holland, Elizabeth Roddy, John McCullen, Fr Martin McAlinden, Carole Leonard, Fr J Nulty, Fr Hugh Connolly, Secretary Episcopal Conference, Fr Liam Holmes, Fr Eugene Sweeney of Ara Coeli and Dr A M McVeigh of the PRONI.

Thanks especially to my wife Rose, a valuable literary critic and counsel, and to our children Niall, Conor and Celine for their patience and skills in unravelling the technical vagaries of the capricious PC.

None of these people has any responsibility for the content, text or any errors or omissions for which I alone take full responsibility

Peter and Maureen Nugent

Abbreviations

North   Northern Ireland

South   Republic of Ireland

CMAC   Catholic Marriage Advisory Council

EPR   Education for Personal Relationships

NMGC   National Marriage Guidance Council

INE   Irish National Executive (1969-1975).

IFFLP   International Federation for Family Life Promotion

NEC   National Executive Committee (from 1975)

CSE   Certificate in Secondary Education (North)

CSWB   Catholic Social Welfare Bureau

CTS   Catholic Truth Society

GCSE   General Certificate in Secondary Education (North)

NFP   Natural Family Planning

BBT   Basal Body Temperature

WCC   Westminster Cathedral Chronicle

WREC   Westminster Religious Education Council

WHO   World Health Organisation

The Graham-Greens

Foreword

CMAC (now Accord) was set up in our diocese of Killaloe in 1969. I was privileged to have been involved in the Ennis centre from then until 1994 when I was appointed bishop. The experience was deeply enriching. The friendship and support of counsellor colleagues was affirming; pre-marriage work with young couples deeply in love with each other was challenging; the privileged access to the deep pain involved in marriage breakdown was humbling.

It is therefore with a profound sense of gratitude that I welcome this story of the early years of CMAC/Accord Ireland. And who better to record that story than Philip Leonard? Even though CMAC was still in its infancy when Killaloe came on stream, Philip was – as we saw him – a veteran counsellor. He was involved from the beginning – at the birth of Newry centre, during the growing years when CMAC in Ireland was still subject to the parent body in London, in the separation of parent and child as CMAC Ireland became independent. Later he became regional director of CMAC Northern Ireland. Philip Leonard was one of the real parents of CMAC Ireland. As a parent it is not always easy to be objective, as indeed he admits in his preface. He writes with an obvious sense of love and commitment to the organisation. He has however done a very professional job in researching and assembling his material.

Through CMAC/Accord married people took ownership of the task of the church's ministry to marriage. In doing so it was being true to the ideas set forth in Vatican II which invited the laity to fuller participation in the life of the church. It was also responding to the mood of the time. Marriage up to then was a very private matter between husband and wife. Difficulties were to be endured. Breakdown was not a matter for discussion. We were gradually emerging from all that silence and beginning to realise that honest open discussion of human relationships was in fact both legitimate and necessary.

I wholeheartedly welcome this personal and unique story of its first quarter of a century of service to the Irish people.

Philip Leonard has already made a significant contribution to the growth and development of CMAC/Accord. He has now greatly added to that contribution by recording the history of those early years.

⊕ *Willie Walsh*
Bishop of Killaloe

Preface

This history is aimed primarily at people coming into Accord, the marriage counselling service in the Catholic Church, that they may have an opportunity to know something of the roots of the organisation and how it spread out its shoots from London in 1946 to every corner of Ireland. Others too may want to know something of the growth of this service to marriage and family in the church; not least those amongst the generations of counsellors who have quietly come and gone over the years, having ministered 'according to the gifts that each has received'.

Fr Andy Kennedy had asked me on a number of occasions to compile the material for a history of the CMAC. For various reasons I declined but, at the end of 1995, after some hesitation, I accepted the invitation of the then Director of Accord, Fr Dan Cavanagh, on behalf of the National Executive to write a history of the organisation. It seemed a good idea to start while some of the founders were still available. Sadly two of those, who were at the centre of things in the early years and who were most helpful to me, have since died. They were co-founder Mrs Eirene Graham-Green, and the priest-director who presided through the years of dramatic growth, Canon Maurice O'Leary.

It might of course be argued that history is best written at a distance, and preferably by a bystander. Contemporary history written from the inside is bound to be biased, tainted with nostalgia and undue regard for old friends. On the other hand, I take comfort from the fact that all history, however objectively written, is essentially the view of the writer who spins a yarn from subjectively selected strands.

This small book has no pretensions to be a comprehensive work, but rather a pocket version, hopefully more readable, written from the vantage point of many years as a voluntary counsellor and later as a fulltime administrator in the organisation. Biestek[1] had a problem in analysing the elements of such a 'living pulsating thing' as the casework relationship. I had a similar difficulty in reducing to cold facts my experience of friends selected for their warmth and quality of caring. This is the story of how these people formed a link with the clergy to become a dynamic and potent movement in the community of the church. It seems appropriate, therefore, to relate the story largely in terms of the people I have identified as key players, who made a special contribution.

This account ends with the departure of Fr Andy Kennedy as Director in 1984. I have added four short histories of the development of the main divisions of the CMAC work in the earlier years. In the interest of brevity, the chapters on the 'Irish Bishops' and 'The Kennedy Years' are abridged versions of original drafts which have been put on ice along with other source material and correspondence, for the benefit of a future student or historian who may write a more inclusive volume.

The title, *Like Ministering to Like*, is taken from *Humanae Vitae*, section 26, 'Family apostolate'.

The Author (Photo by Matt Nolan)

Introduction

The history of this marriage counselling service in the church is remarkable for two reasons. Firstly, its founding was due entirely to the initiative of the Catholic bishops and their priests and, secondly, it opened the way for the recruitment of a small army of lay people into pastoral work in the area of marriage and family, truly a lay apostolate in the terms of *Humanae Vitae* – married people ministering to one another. The establishment of the marriage counselling service activated a renewed concern in the church for the welfare of Christian marriage – what it is that undermines it, and what sustains, together with a renewed interest in marriage as a sacrament, and the development of a theology of marriage.

Accord, as the service is now known in Ireland ('Marriage Care' in Britain), derived from the Catholic Marriage Advisory Council of Britain and Ireland. From its introduction in Belfast in 1962 it has grown into a major pastoral service in the Irish church. The reason for this is tragically simple: a high proportion of marriages, including Catholic marriages, get into trouble, many ending in breakdown. In marriage, as in life, there is illness and premature death. Accord is a marriage health service; the divorce court is a marriage graveyard.

Marriage breakdown is invariably a most distressing human experience. Only those who have been there know the full degree of the loneliness and pain. The sense of failure is all pervasive – to Catholics in particular who feel guilty on two counts: not only have they failed the marriage, but they have also failed the grace of the sacrament. As a consequence, Catholics in the past have been more reluctant to accept that they had a problem and to seek help. This is now changing.

Conflict in marriage is natural and, in a healthy marriage, is worked out in the security of mutual respect and trust. Unfortunately it can also deteriorate into persistent conflict which, if unresolved, may degenerate into a state referred to as 'chronic disharmony'. At this stage, the potential of the marriage to heal, to affirm and to build, flips to the opposite: the marriage becomes a wasteland of insecurity where there is confusion, anxiety and a destructive anger which eats at the heart long after the marriage has ended.

Accord's first concern is to heal the wounded. Contrary to a common misconception, its main purpose is not the saving of marriages but the saving of people. The counsellors provide a listening ear and help the client to restore self confidence and self esteem. The service is voluntary. No one is turned away. To be able to help someone in this sensitive area calls for special personal qualities and skills. This is why Accord, in common with other marriage counselling agencies, has a stringent selection process and a long period of intensive training before a counsellor is qualified to practice.

As a marriage counselling agency Accord is unique in the effort devoted to marriage preparation. No other organisation attracts so many couples to pre-marriage courses. This is not to say that pre-marriage courses are the key to marriage success; only the most naïve would imagine that the way to be successfully married can be learned in a few easy lessons. However, attendance at such courses is at least an acknowledgement by couples that marriage brings problems and that this is an opportunity to see how such problems arise and how to be prepared for them – in other words an opportunity to attain a more realistic expectation of marriage and of the effort required to make it work.

Dr Jack Dominian describes marriage breakdown and divorce as 'the most important social evil in western society'.[1] While the number of marriages in Ireland remains constant, the number of breakdowns is unfortunately increasing. In the words of a Home Office report in 1979, 'marriage was never more popular, never more risky'.[2] So long as there are marriages there will be marriage problems, and Accord and similar organisations will be a feature of our society.

Dr Jim Barnes

*Dr Raymond McGill
with his grandaughter Sonya.*

Professor John Marshall

Dr Jack Dominian

The Catholic Marriage Advisory Council

MINUTES of the FIRST MEETING

of the Advisory Committee held on Tuesday 26 February 1946
at 5 p.m.

PRESENT

     Mr.Graham J. Graham-Green (Chairman)

     Lady Holberton for Mrs.Given-Wilson

     Mrs.Everest

     Hon. Mrs.Bower

     Mr.Richard O'Sullivan K.C.

     Rt.Revd.Mgr. H. Beauchamp V.G.

     Mr. A.J.Tressidder

CHAIRMAN

     After a motion proposed by Mr.Richard O'Sullivan and
seconded by Mrs.Bower Mr.Graham-Green was unanimously elected
chairman.

BUSINESS

1.   Aims and Objects

       A report on the Aims and Objects of the Council was
made by the Chairman and accepted by the Committee. The
Chairman also read correspondence with His Grace the
Archbishop of Westminster showing that the Council had
His Grace's unqualified approval

2.   Title

       It was unanimously decided that the title of
"Catholic Marriage Advisory Council" should be adopted

An extract from the minutes of the first meeting of the CMAC

CHAPTER 1

Genesis

The CMAC was the brainchild of a remarkable London couple, Major Graham J Graham-Green and his wife Eirene. Their lasting contribution was to institute, in 1946, a service of the highest professional standards on a sound legal basis as a national organisation which attracted the recognition and support of government.

Backdrop
Accord actually had its origins in the British army. The parent organisation, the Catholic Marriage Advisory Council, was the brainchild of a Catholic officer, Major Graham John Graham-Green. A lawyer in civilian life, his duties in the aftermath of the second world war included helping troops in London with marriage problems. He came to the conclusion that there should be a separate organisation for Catholic personnel. By coincidence his wife Eirene, a social worker, had arrived at the same conclusion for Catholic civilians. He approached Cardinal Griffin who authorised them to form such an organisation and so the CMAC was founded. In the beginning senior army officers figured largely in its activities; the first CMAC pre-marriage courses in London in 1948 were exclusively for army personnel with the approval of the Commander of London District, Brigadier Trappes-Lomax, (referred to by Graham-Green as a 'well known Catholic')[1] who was persuaded by Brigadier J G Frere, then Secretary of the National Office of the CMAC.

The CMAC began as a distinctly upper-class organisation. The list of members of the first Executive Committee, as one observer wryly commented, looks like a Catholic Debrett! What is manifest is that these influential Catholics gave generously of their time and effort in the work of the church. They carried some weight in society, not least in government circles, and obviously had the confidence of Cardinal Griffin who entrusted them with this sensitive pastoral work, an heroic step on his part at that time.

Counselling at that time was perceived as giving advice and guidance (hence the name) and therefore appropriate to professional people and others recognised as qualified to act in this capacity. The first members of the CMAC referred to themselves not as counsellors, but as 'consultants'. Within a few years came Carl Rogers, with his theory of therapy based on the relationship between counsellor and client, and on the counsellor's acceptance of and respect and care for the client. His theory revolutionised the perception of counselling, of the qualities required in a counsellor, and the training required. Elements from the comparatively new field of psychotherapy entered into the basic training. Gradually these changes were reflected in the make-up of people recruited and of those who succeeded the first generation at headquarters.

The Graham-Greens – Founders of the CMAC
Major Graham Graham-Green (no relation to Graham Green the author) had been posted to the Judge Advocate General's Department because of his legal background. The war over, he was placed in charge of a 'loose organisation' within the army, charged with giving troops advice on the many marriage problems that had arisen. His wife Eirene, meanwhile, trained as a social worker by the Citizen's Advice Bureau and operating in a deprived area of London, found herself very much engaged in advising and comforting people in similar difficulties. Gradually the Graham-Greens became convinced that there ought to be an organisation for Catholics seeking help with marriage problems and that much marital unhappiness could have been avoided had there been an organisation to help at an early stage. What Graham-Green had in mind then was some provision for army personnel, but eventually found the solution in the form of a new organisation within the church.

At first the Graham-Greens were hesitant to promote their ideas. The notion of a lay organisation to deal specifically with Catholic marriage problems was totally new 'not only to Catholics but to the world at large'. Hitherto the Catholic clergy 'regarded themselves as the proper persons to advise their parishioners on any marriage problems that might arise'. When the Graham-Greens tried out their ideas on clerical friends they got little encouragement. One senior Catholic chaplain said the ideas were excellent but 'you will never get them accepted'. Then something happened to trigger them into action: the announcement of the opening, in London, of new offices for the National Marriage Guidance Council (the NMGC). Graham-Green wrote: 'When my wife saw this she realised at once her ideas had been right. The result was that as soon as I was released from the army my wife insisted on the problem being put to the fountain head, the Cardinal Archbishop of Westminster. With some trepidation I wrote to that great and kindly priest, Cardinal Bernard Griffin, asking him for an audience. To my great surprise and joy, after hearing our suggestions he said to me, "We will have a Catholic Marriage Council" but then, to my utter consternation, he said, "Go ahead and form it. I can't give you much money but you may use my name as you think fit."'

What Graham-Green apparently did not know was that his visit to the Cardinal in January 1946 followed on an earlier visit to his Eminence by Dr David Mace, Director of NMGC, in a chance combination of events which would lead to the formation of the CMAC.

The NMGC, which was founded in 1938, had suspended operations when war broke out in 1939, but resumed work towards the end of the war in response to the increasing incidence of marriage breakdown. Dr Mace had visited the Cardinal to explain that they were having difficulties dealing with Catholics, and to suggest a specially recruited and trained branch of NMGC to meet the needs of Catholic clients. Graham-Green's proposal for a marriage counselling service in the church was most timely, and the Cardinal obviously saw it as the answer to the problem.

A Prototype
As Graham-Green recovered from the shock of the Cardinal's directive, the picture took shape. There was nothing in the church by way of a model but it was clear that this must be a totally Catholic organisation to which Catholics could turn with

confidence. The NMGC advocated birth control, and this Graham-Green knew would be entirely out of the question in a Catholic organisation. Nevertheless, he turned to Dr Mace and found him most sympathetic and helpful, so that the two organisations were subsequently 'able to work openly in mutual harmony'. Graham-Green modelled the CMAC structure on the NMGC, even adapting the name with the approval of Dr Mace.[2] The NMGC apparently also helped with training. One member, Fred Wells-Pestell, a social worker from Oxford and subsequently a life-peer and Parliamentary Secretary in the Department of Health and Social Security, told Bernard Cawley, then one of his advisors in the department, that he had a hand in the early training of CMAC counsellors.

From the first, Graham-Green envisaged a national organisation which would extend from the London headquarters throughout the country, with branches 'in every diocese and in every city of importance'. This raised the questions of finance, of head office accommodation, of finding suitable people to do the work and training them, and of instituting procedures in accordance with the highest standards of case-work practice. His wife Eirene recalls: 'We were given rent-free offices by a Jewish businessman in Parliament Square. I, as the first Chief Counsellor, set about finding furniture to equip the offices, and recruited Catholics as volunteers, all married, whom I trained, as my experience as chief adviser to the Citizens Advice Bureaux gave me the correct insight into the root and not the apparent cause of marital breakdowns.'[3]

Eirene acted as Chief Counsellor until it became possible to appoint a fulltime social worker. The counsellors were assisted by specialists, priests, doctors, and lawyers.

The Legal Basis

As a lawyer himself Graham-Green recognised an immediate need: 'It must have a permanent constitution. Committees dissolve, individuals die, so there must be a company as a permanent organisation. A company limited by guarantee, without share capital and without the word "limited" in its name, was incorporated on 19 August 1946, and this is the company which has stood the passing of time and today is your parent body.'

Government Recognition

There was yet another mountain to climb. The government had appointed a committee under Lord (then Mr Justice) Denning to advise on the best method of stemming the mounting tide of divorce cases. It became clear that the committee would probably regard one marriage counselling organisation as adequate for the country, regardless of creed. Nevertheless, they agreed to accept a memorandum from CMAC. Graham-Green's foresight in establishing CMAC as a national body, which drew criticism at the time, now became evident. He knew that no government grant would be available unless the service was available throughout the entire country. In Marshall's words: 'It was therefore essential to secure the agreement of all the bishops to centres being established in their dioceses. Graham-Green asked permission to address the bishops at their 1947 Low Week meeting. Cardinal Griffin thought this was not practical but agreed to put a memorandum before the meeting. Graham-Green produced a hard hitting memorandum, addressing the bishops in terms to which they were not accustomed. He pointed out that they all must agree; there must be no 'no-go areas'; if one diocese opted out then all would lose the money. The problem for the bishops was that the care of married people was seen as a pastoral concern, the province of the priest ... It was not an area in which lay people had hitherto been involved. Priests would need to be convinced that lay-people could be helpful in this field. Despite these concerns the bishops agreed.' (M 12)

Graham-Green recalled: 'Seeing the way things were going, I begged Lord Denning to hear our Cardinal put the case for a separate Catholic body and so it was agreed and a day fixed. As a result, the Denning Committee in their Report recommended that marriage guidance should be encouraged and financial grants given in aid and that Catholics should be entitled to have their own organisation. '

The Report was accepted by the government and the Harris Committee set up to determine the appropriate grants. By the end of 1947 CMAC had been awarded a substantial grant for an experimental period of five years.

Clerical Support

The Home Office package included a place for a representative of the CMAC on a new training board, a government grant of 75% of the cost of the Central Office, plus additional grants towards training. For the rest, Graham-Green had to look to the church. Alas, the support was not forthcoming. Marshall writes: 'The purse strings were firmly in the hands of the clergy who (apart from Cardinal Griffin) did not respond to the call for help for this lay-run organisation'. (M 20) This, together with the lack of success in establishing centres outside London, undoubtedly contributed to Graham-Green's decision that he should be succeeded by a priest.

Marshall continues: 'Securing the Home Office grant was a great achievement on the part of Graham-Green. He had recognised the opportunity, not only to obtain money but, perhaps of more importance, to secure recognition for a Catholic organisation in this field. He had made strong representations to Lord Denning, persuaded Cardinal Griffin of the need to appear before the enquiry in person, and secured the agreement of the entire hierarchy. This achievement was to have far-reaching effects, particularly by enabling CMAC, through its membership of the training board, to participate fully in many developments in marriage counselling which were taking place.' (M 12)

History, it is said, is made by unforeseen consequences. The concept of CMAC, Graham writes, resulted from a combination of 'unrelated events'. His wife's involvement with social work (were it not for a family illness she would have been at university); his own army posting to work on marriage problems; the opening of the new NMGC offices at the vital moment. But it was the Graham-Greens themselves who were central to the outcome. They had the perception to recognise the opportunity, together with the energy and initiative to do something about it. But for them CMAC would not exist. As Marshall comments: 'it is very doubtful that an enterprise of this kind would ever have been started by the official church'. (M20)

Professionalism

From the beginning the Graham-Greens insisted on the highest standards. They introduced the unique selection system (based

on a War Office system of selecting officers) which remains unchanged today. They were assiduous in writing up case notes,
instituted monthly meetings 'as essential to training since they
gave counsellors an opportunity of learning from one another'
and, in accordance with the Cardinal's wishes, founded the pre-
marriage courses. 'It was obvious that prevention was much better than cure; that whilst the immediate necessity was to mend
marriages we must proceed with courses on preparation for
marriage.' Today the pre-marriage courses are a feature of the
CMAC's service in Britain and in Ireland.

Graham-Green served as chairman for five years before illness forced his retirement. 'I had been pressing the Cardinal for
some time to appoint a priest who could devote his full time to
the work of the Council but it was not until I had a severe operation and wanted a rest that he acceded to my request.' In 1951,
after five years in control, Cardinal Griffin appointed Fr Robert
Gorman SJ to succeed Graham-Green.

Graham Green was a man of action and of humanity and
faith. In an address at the service of thanksgiving for his life and
work, Chief Master Horne said of Graham-Green: 'He was
above all a most kindly and compassionate man whose
Christian faith sustained him in every aspect of his daily life and
whose concern for his fellow men was expressed in all his
numerous activities.'[4]

He lived to see the organisation he founded established in
virtually every diocese in England, Wales, Scotland and Ireland
and recognised everywhere for its professionalism and the emphasis on high standards. His last recorded words on CMAC,
published after his death were: '... how very pleased I am to see,
in the recent development of the Council, all my dreams come to
fruition.'

CHAPTER 2

Cardinal Griffin 1899-1956
Patron of the CMAC

Cardinal Griffin had a strong sense of the potential of Catholics in the community as a lay apostolate. It was consistent with this belief that he should entrust this sensitive pastoral work in the area of marriage and family to a group of lay people, an unprecedented development in the church at that time

A Man of Action

Cardinal Griffin was obviously a man of vision. He was also a man in a hurry. Perhaps he had a premonition that his time was short. When he was raised to Cardinal at the relatively young age of 47 he had but 10 years to live, years dogged by a series of heart attacks. He was, in modern parlance, a 'workaholic', intolerant of procrastination and time-consuming procedures. Once he came to a decision he was quick to act. After his death, Bishop Beck of Salford wrote of him, 'he was not given to be patient with committees and with long-winded consideration of administrative questions. He preferred, whenever possible, to make personal decisions or to make a single person responsible for a particular field of diocesan activity'.[1]

This is exactly what he did when he gave the go-ahead for the CMAC. Having reached his decision to accede to Graham-Green's request to institute a marriage counselling service in the church, he promptly authorised Graham-Green and his wife to set it up in his name. This was a radical decision on two counts: firstly to involve lay people in pastoral work in the area of marriage and family, hitherto the prerogative of the clergy, and secondly to place a lay person in charge. At the time he had two private secretaries, one of whom was the future Archbishop Derek Warlock, who was widely regarded as being closely involved in the Cardinal's decision.

In those days, marriage problems were regarded by Catholics, especially clergy, as to some degree a failure on the part of the couple to fully realise the grace of sacrament, and therefore properly a matter for the priest in his role as spiritual director. Bernard Cawley (later to become a Director of CMAC) writes: 'Seen in this context it must be regarded as quite extraordinary that even such a young Archbishop as Griffin then was, could have agreed to such a revolutionary step as to found the CMAC, sixteen years before Pope John decided to open the church's windows to fresh air.'[2]

The Reluctant Clergy

The obvious danger was an adverse reaction in the clerical ranks. The Cardinal was sensitive to their feelings. Professor John Marshall says of him, 'He clearly was a man of vision but he saw there would be difficulties with the clergy. In his first address to the annual conference of the CMAC he tackled the issue head on. He said he was glad to see the clergy there. He wanted to reassure them that CMAC was not trying to take over their bailiwick but they were there to help.'[3] Marshall records, as an encouraging feature, that of the referrals to the London centre by the end of 1946, two-thirds had been referred by parish priests. (M 10) Nevertheless, outside London the evidence is that there was for some years a marked resistance to introduce this new service in the dioceses. Marshall again: 'The lay founders of the CMAC had succeeded in London because they had the backing of Cardinal Griffin and because the size and anonymity of the metropolis meant they could operate independently of the clergy. But as soon as they endeavoured to move to other places where the Catholic community was more closely knit, the way was blocked. If CMAC was to spread it had to come under clerical control. '(M 24)

Father Robert Gorman SJ, who was appointed by the Cardinal to succeed Graham-Green as chairman in 1951, made the breakthrough in establishing some centres outside London, but it was not until Father (later Canon) O'Leary became chairman in 1956 that the CMAC began to find widespread acceptance amongst the clergy.

A Nationwide Organisation

In Graham-Green the Cardinal found the right man to lay the foundations for an organisation that would extend far beyond the boundaries of the Westminster archdiocese, as he clearly intended. When Father O'Leary took up the post of chairman, the Cardinal urged him to visit all the bishops in the country to explain the purpose of the CMAC and to place his services at their disposal. This Father O'Leary proceeded to do. Very soon he found his mission extended to Ireland.

One of Cardinal Griffin's important contributions to the CMAC was his personal appearance before the Denning Committee at the request of Graham-Green. His progressive outlook was further reflected in approving research to be conducted into natural methods of contraception at a time when even legitimate methods of birth control were regarded with misgivings in the Catholic community. (M 103)

An Educated Lay Apostolate

In his last years the Cardinal had a strong sense of the role of an educated laity as a lay apostolate – a description he had come to prefer to the words 'Catholic Action' 'which, in the past, have often meant either a paper organisation or action which is more active than Catholic'.[4] Addressing Catholic undergraduates at Cambridge in 1955, he referred to an increasing emphasis on the role of the laity but stressed the need for adequate formation and training: 'If our apostolate is to be effective we must be equipped for our role. This involves training – spiritual, doctrinal and professional ... The lay apostolate without adequate formation and training can even be dangerous. During recent years we have urged our Catholic organisations to be active in the training of their members.'[5]

Ever since his early days in Birmingham when he was administrator of the Hudson Homes for children (he once claimed that he had 687 children in his care, from 3 months to 18 years), he had a concern with the welfare of the family. Canon O'Leary recalls as a young priest being present at a meeting called by the Cardinal to consider ideas for family support. When the Graham-Greens presented their proposal to him he obviously saw it as an important opportunity in this area. He lived to see his trust in this lay organisation fully justified and its potential realised. Canon O'Leary recalls in his last conversation with him that the Cardinal expressed his high regard for the CMAC and his great wish to see it extended.

A special number of the *Westminster Cathedral Chronicle* of November 1956, devoted entirely to obituaries, makes no mention of the CMAC, possibly his most enduring memorial!

In a contribution to his obituaries, Monsignor (later Archbishop) Warlock referred to the late Cardinal's love for France, because of his devotion to Saint Térèse of Lisieux, and also to his love for Ireland. In his last illness he was very disappointed to have to abandon his plans for his annual holiday to 'his beloved County Kerry'.[6]

Cardinal Bernard Griffin

Cardinal Griffin was born in Birmingham on 21 February 1899 and had a twin brother, a Benedictine, Dom Basil, and three younger sisters, one a nun. His parents, devout Catholics, were both city councillors. His father was a businessman. In 1918, the last year of the first world war, his studies were interrupted when he was called to active service in the Royal Naval Air Service. In that year he developed rheumatic fever with cardiac complications. He was ordained in 1924, appointed Auxiliary Bishop of Birmingham and Vicar General of the diocese in 1938, Archbishop of Westminster in 1943, and Cardinal in 1946. He died in Cornwall on 20 August 1956.

CHAPTER 3

Fr Gorman
First Priest Chairman (1951-1956)

The appointment of a priest as chairman by Cardinal Griffin was a tactical move, at the request of Graham-Green, to win the confidence of the clergy outside Westminster.

A Clerical Coup

Graham-Green, who resigned as chairman in July 1951 because of ill health, was succeeded for a few months by Sir Harold Hood Bt. Graham-Green's request to be succeeded by a priest was granted in October 1951, when Fr Robert C Gorman took over as Chairman. There is, however, some evidence that there was more to Fr Gorman's appointment than a simple response to Graham-Green's wishes.

Arising from a complaint about something that was said at a CMAC marriage preparation course in which Brigadier Frere, a member of the executive committee, was involved, the committee received a letter from Archbishop Myers, Auxiliary at Westminster, enquiring into its composition. The Archbishop expressed the view 'that the executive committee should be strengthened and that a rota of priests should be drawn up who would be present whenever moral theology, as distinct from psychology and physiology, was being taught'. (M 19) (The letter was received on 21 June with a request for a reply by 2 July.) The takeover was like a military coup. Marshall writes: 'Any consultations that took place are not recorded but, on 18 October 1951, Fr R C Gorman attended a meeting of the executive committee for the first time and informed them that he had been appointed chairman of the national headquarters and of the London centre by Cardinal Griffin. Fr Gorman was a Jesuit from Farm Street who was trained in psychology. He arrived at the meeting with a list of (five) new members for the executive committee – all were made members of the company and then appointed members of the executive committee. At the next meeting on 29 November, F A Butcher, the treasurer, and Brigadier Frere, formerly general secretary, both resigned; no reasons were recorded in the minutes.' (M 19)

Graham-Green, however, remained on the committee until June 1953 when a legal appointment made it impossible for him to continue.

The Breakthrough

Fr Gorman proved himself to be an effective new broom. He immediately tightened procedures in the interest of confidentiality.[1] A trained psychologist, he acted as tutor and raised the standard of training to a more professional level. He extended his control of the organisation by having members of the executive appointed to the London centre committee and to the medical panel. But his most outstanding achievement was the breakthrough in having the first centres established outside London. He made the rounds of bishops and priests to such effect that, when he left after four and a half years, five centres were in operation outside London and a number were in the pipeline. Marshall considers it self evident that this achievement was due to his being a priest. In the Graham-Green years, a member of the committee, Sir Henry Digby-Beste, 'had given an enormous amount of time to seeing bishops and priests in the effort to establish new centres' to no avail. (M 21)

Concomitant with this development was the welcome appearance of financial contributions from dioceses other than Westminster which, until then, had been meeting the full costs of the church's contribution to the organisation. The result was a constant struggle to survive, lurching, as Marshall says, 'from one financial crisis to another, being repeatedly saved by one generous, usually anonymous, donor or another'. (M 18) Their difficulties were compounded in March 1952 when the Home Office reduced the rate of grant from 75% to 50% 'because it felt too little was being done by the Catholic community to support the work'. (M 21) Under Fr Gorman things began to improve: 'There was more willingness to give to a priest than to a lay person.' (M 21) The improvement must have been relative because when Fr O'Leary took over from Fr Gorman in February 1956, he found the organisation bankrupt.

Left CMAC in Better Shape

Like Graham-Green before him, ill health forced Fr Gorman to retire. Perhaps inevitably his time of control was marked by what Marshall calls the 'clericalisation' of the organisation. All the new centres except one had a priest as chairman which gave rise to the office of 'priest chairman', a feature of the organisation for many years. One consequence of this clericalisation was the loss of the former closeness with the NMGC and a degree of strain with the Home Office. But undoubtedly Gorman's chairmanship years brought great progress. In Marshall's words: 'CMAC was in better shape than it had been five years before and was well placed for the next move forward.' (M 21)

Major Graham John Graham-Green CB., TD., FCIArb., (1907-1985) and Eirene (1907-1997)

Founder chairman of the CMAC with the approval of Cardinal Bernard Griffin, Archbishop of Westminster, in August 1946. A solicitor by profession, he served in the Honourable Artillery Company in the war. After many years of private practice he served as Master of the Supreme Court of Judicature for almost twenty years before he being appointed Chief Taxing Master in 1972, a post he carried out until his retirement in 1979. Author of many standard works on legal practice, Graham-Green became a Freeman of the City of London in 1945 and in his later years the founder chairman of the Board of Trustees of the Friends of Osborne House where he was for some time a patient.

His wife Eirene, whom he credits with being the first to have the idea of a Catholic marriage counselling agency, 'and to whom the credit for the Council really belongs' was an able partner in the foundation years. Their daughter, Veronica, holds a finance appointment in the MOD and is an officer in the Royal Auxiliary Air Force.

Graham-Green died 22 August 1985. Eirene died 4 January 1997.

CHAPTER 4

Canon Maurice P O'Leary,
Chairman/Director CMAC (1956-1974)
and expansion into Ireland

This very English priest with the Irish name was destined to take the CMAC tide at the flood. In his eighteen years of leadership he saw the service established countrywide in Britain and Ireland.

A Leader Appears

The organisation had been running for almost ten years when, in February 1956, Cardinal Griffin appointed a successor to the ailing Fr Gorman. He was Father (later Canon) Maurice O'Leary, a curate in London who was destined to lead the CMAC for the next 18 years, a period in which it would grow from uncertain beginnings into an established pastoral service in Britain and Ireland. At the end of his first year there were 8 centres in operation in England. When he left there were more than 100, of which over 30 were in Ireland. He chaired every selection conference (over 300 in all) and had a hand in setting up every centre, which gave him an intimate knowledge of the personnel in the organisation. It was a development of astonishing proportions in which the physical growth of the CMAC was matched with a corresponding growth in its professionalism and its spiritual basis. He made an enormous contribution through his leadership, his tireless energy and not least his ability to attract and keep a core of highly qualified people around him at headquarters.

At first acquaintance the Canon showed little evidence of the ebullient qualities frequently associated with leadership. Slight of figure, reflective and softly spoken, with a disarming smile, he was reticent to the point of diffidence. His most noticeable feature was the pallor of his face and complete baldness suggesting a past illness, never mentioned. In his clerical black he was a striking figure and distinguished by a little black skull-cap worn

33

at all times. He had an impish sense of humour and took a mis-
chievous pleasure in the unspoken curiosity of people at the
sight of this ever present calotte. There was one exception: he
liked to tell how a waitress in Dublin once approached him saying she had been sent by the kitchen staff to ask him a question.
He knew immediately what it was. 'Why do you wear that little
black cap?' she said. 'Well I have to tell you the truth. It's because I've no hair!'

His somewhat frail appearance belied a tough and durable
character with immense stamina and a quiet assurance which
exuded an inner strength and authority. Marshal attributes this
assurance to the schools he attended, especially the English
College in Rome. 'Most of the bishops and other holders of high
office in the church in England had been students at the English
College. This gave the college an eminence which was reflected
in the assurance and confidence of the students, not unlike that
of English public school boys. Maurice O'Leary had imbibed
this assurance; he met officials at the Home Office and directors
of other organisations as equals and showed no diffidence in
dealing with bishops.' (M 22) Canon O'Leary confirms that the
connections he made in the English College were an advantage.
When, at Cardinal Griffin's request, he made the rounds of the
English bishops to introduce them to the CMAC he found many
of them had connections with the College, '... some of them in
fact I knew because they had visited the college, especially the
ones who were ex-students'.[1] But it was in Ireland that his personal qualities had the greatest effect. He won over the Irish hierarchy and senior clergy totally and, without exception, they
accepted him and the case he made for the CMAC.

A Mysterious Assignment

The Cardinal first mentioned the appointment to Fr O'Leary in
January 1956 when he was a curate in Warwick Street, near
Picadilly Circus. He recalled the Cardinal's words: 'The man
who is doing it wants to get out. He keeps bothering me – says
he can't go on.' Fr O'Leary knew of the CMAC and had done
some work for it, but the Cardinal was unwell and Fr O'Leary
did not realise what work he was being asked to take over. 'I
heard nothing for a few weeks so I somehow got the sense of

false security! By the middle of February I was told to get in touch with Fr Gorman at Farm St Church, and take over from him.' He went to Fr Gorman for a briefing but found him unwilling to impart any information. Fr O'Leary gave up in frustration. 'I couldn't get anything from him!'

When he did take over he got an unpleasant surprise. 'One of the first letters I got was from the bank. The CMAC was bust!' He had to pay the wages out of his own pocket, helped by his PP. The Cardinal, who found this amusing, came across with a substantial cheque.

Road to Damascus

Knowing nothing about counselling, Fr O'Leary began to educate himself. A priest friend lent him two books. One was Carl Rogers' book on non-directive counselling. The other was on counselling and Catholic principles. The result was, for him, something of a road to Damascus.

He began to see counselling as not only in line with his priestly training but 'dependent very much on respect for the person, the dignity of the person, the need for self-awareness, the need for self-knowledge, the need for awe. The standing back and realising it is about this person and God, and nobody can get between this person and God ... There was a whole realm of things here wonderful and mysterious.'[2] He pondered on how he could convey this insight to others. The task became his mission to the organisation which, over the years, he conducted with extraordinary presence and quiet effect. He was destined to be the channel of a new spirit within CMAC.

A Vocation Found

His remit from the Cardinal was simple – to develop CMAC, 'to take it up and down the country and extend it'. This he set out to do in Great Britain and, almost immediately, in response to numerous invitations, in Ireland. But first there was the task of restoring harmony and unity to the organisation at home. Two of the eight centres he inherited had taken umbrage with Central Office requirements and had declared 'UDI'. Because CMAC centres are autonomous under the bishop in each diocese, the authority of Central Office is more accorded by the centre than imposed from above. Nevertheless, Fr O'Leary quickly realised that central control was vital to uniformity of standards and quality of service nation-wide. Breakaway centres would produce a hotchpotch that would undermine efficiency and prestige. He proceeded quietly to bring the errant centres back into the fold.

Fr O'Leary showed remarkable powers of diplomacy, in all situations. Fionnuala Arthur, one of the first CMAC tutors and a selector for many years, attributes this to a natural gift for non-directive counselling. In his account of his discovery of the nature of counselling he makes a significant comment: 'I was able ... to see that this was very much in line with all in which I had been trained, and yet had never realised what it was I had been trained in, particularly in what Thomas Aquinas had been insistent upon: Prudence as a governing virtue, prudence which he defined as *Recta Ratio Agibilium*, in literal translation – the right way of ordering things which may be done.'[3]

The virtue of prudence and 'the right way of ordering things' which he personalised, was to be his staff and his shield through some difficult periods of growth and change. There was quite an evolution in counselling in the years when he was in control and there were parallel advances in other branches of the service – in pre-marriage courses, the schools service and in the natural family planning service. People trained in old models were being asked to adapt to new perceptions, new methods. A group of tutors were specially trained and in-service training encouraged. Annual conferences, which provided an opportunity to hear experts and to digest their theories, were found to be a tremendous stimulus to the morale of the counsellors and to improved performance.

The new ideas inevitably caused tensions between 'traditionalists' and 'modernists' and there were many arguments and debates in the ranks. Such periods of growing pains proved a testing time for the person at the helm. Fr O'Leary's leadership at such times was a model of caring non-intervention. It could be summed up as having faith in the counsellors to adopt whatever course was in the best interest of the client. One of his stalwarts at Central Office was the psychiatrist Dr Jack Dominian, whose new insights into sexuality and marriage were, from the 1960s, causing ripples in church circles. He caused more than a few ripples later when he openly disagreed with *Humanae Vitae*. The CMAC was a useful platform and again Fr O'Leary did not intervene as Dominian's biographer acknowledges: 'Dominian believes that three men made it possible for him to communicate his vision of sexuality and marriage to the wider world. The first was Maurice O'Leary who, as chairman of CMAC, gave him total freedom within the organisation for twenty years.'[4]

Mission to Ireland

After initial visits to Dublin and Belfast in 1956, there was no movement until Belfast got going in 1962. Thereafter throughout the 1960s, Fr O'Leary's CMAC work in Ireland became something of an odyssey in the land of his fathers – giving information meetings, presiding at selection conferences, advising on the basic training. 'The time was ripe. Nothing could be done without the understanding of the bishops. I had to have faith in them and they in me. It was a two-way process. I used to say I was like St Patrick being invited to come back to Ireland, but nobody believed me!' There were over 30 centres in Ireland by the time Fr O'Leary retired in 1974, all being serviced from Westminster. (Ireland did not go independent until the following year.) He found in Ireland (and in Scotland) 'a paternalism on the part of the clergy – they were very protective – and they protected particularly the fertile wives. They were very conscious that these ladies should be at home with their children and shouldn't be enticed out. I used to tell them that these women have got minds of their own ... They won't thank you for not considering them for this work.'

He had a remarkable personal impact in Ireland. 'I think I got in the door with the "O'Leary" ... they were surprised when they heard the English accent. But they didn't throw me out. I was a bit of a fraud!' He enjoys telling how, in Kilkenny, a taxi-driver took him in mistake to the house of the Protestant Bishop. 'Well you talk like a Protestant, Sir,' the man explained. There were, of course, a few Irish hiccups. Fionnuala Arthur remembers an information meeting when the visitors were relating some of the bizarre things people get up to in problem marriages in England. A local psychiatrist jumped up exclaiming, 'We don't have people like that in Ireland!' and stomped out of the room.

Then there was that famous occasion at another information meeting in a college, to which some of the students were admitted. In Fr O'Leary's words, 'At the end of the proceedings a man stood up and made a most impassioned speech ... I didn't understand a word of it because he spoke in Irish. I knew something was going on because all the doctors, priests and lay people looked rather uncomfortable but the students were laughing their heads off. So, when he had finished and the students had finished cheering and whilst everyone else kept very quiet, I ask the doctor beside me what he had said. He replied, 'Well, he summed it up in the last sentence. He really was talking to you. He told you to go back where you came from, and leave the women of Ireland alone!'[5]

The idea that this benign, quiet-voiced, urbane priest was really a Machiavelli come from England to lure the holy women of Ireland into dangerous paths clearly left the adult audience speechless. The students obviously found it hilarious! Fortunately the bishops and the Irish clergy had no such reservations. They trusted Fr O'Leary and, in his own words, 'the time was ripe'. His mission to Ireland was a memorable success.

His first and most important 'conquest' amongst the bishops was Archbishop McQuaid of Dublin 'whom I revered and loved and feel so grateful to for his kindness and for his great wisdom'.[6] His second was Bishop Daniel Mageean in Belfast who 'was very friendly, kindly and he did approve'.[7] Amongst the many friends he made in Ireland he had a special regard for Fr Michael Browne who was chairman in the early days in Dublin and was later involved in setting up CMAC Ireland. 'I was greatly taken to Michael and had a great regard for him. He never obtruded, never said this is how it must be done. He was one of the wisest priests I ever met. The bishops trusted him.'

Cometh the Hour, Cometh the Man

When the time came to intervene, Fr O'Leary responded with all the authority of the born leader. The occasion was the publication of *Humanae Vitae* in 1968. To the dismay of those in the Catholic community who had hoped and expected that the contraceptive pill would be declared acceptable, the document forbade all forms of artificial contraception. Thereupon a debate began between those who would not question the authority of the Pope and would follow the letter of the law, and those who advocated tempering the teaching by the exercise of private conscience. The CMAC personnel, married people themselves and closely concerned with the problems of marriage and family, were particularly affected. Many counsellors shared the anger and confusion.

The 1968 annual conference at Keele University, which followed the publication of the document within a matter of weeks, was in danger of disintegrating into a free-for-all. Fr O'Leary's performance as chairman was superb. When the document appeared he immediately issued a letter to all counsellors to restore a sense of calm and direction, acknowledging the hurt and bewilderment around but reminding them of their commitment to help others: 'We work together in the CMAC serving in our different ways those who are married and who will marry, and trying above all to enable them to understand the wonder and demands of love. Can we show that we ourselves are a true community of love, sensitive to each other's needs, and still concerned for the needs of those we have come together to serve?'[8]

It proved to be a memorable conference in the evolution of the CMAC. Devoted entirely to the encyclical, the main speakers were Monsignor Alan C Clark who, with the Reverend Geoffrey Crawford, had translated the encyclical from the Latin text, and Dr Denis O'Callaghan, Professor of Moral Theology at Maynooth, who was remembered for his address on 'The Evolving Theology of Marriage' to the first residential conference two years before. Clark, sombre and balanced, presented the document as the authoritative teaching of the church. The faithful had a duty to accept and not to question. O'Callaghan, effervescent as always, agreed that the encyclical expressed the principles of church teaching, but that its application in practice demanded pastoral sensitivity in human situations where couples experience particular difficulties.

Fr O'Leary's earlier circular had forearmed the counsellors. He continued in the same vein at the conference, reminding his listeners that, as non-directive counsellors, their task was to help their clients by enabling them to reach their own responsible decisions. Their own personal views were irrelevant to that consideration but the presence of such views must be expected: 'It would be remarkable if anyone who has a special concern for marriage and family should feel unaffected ... (but) it is not help-ful to complicate and endanger the counselling relationship by declaring one's own personal position to the client and perhaps one's own intellectual and emotional difficulties.'[9] In the words of Bernard Cawley, later Chief Executive of the CMAC, 'if Maurice did nothing else for CMAC and the community at large, and manifestly he did far more than that, he would de-serve our undying gratitude for this reminder.'[10]

A New Beginning

Rather than dividing on the issues, the conference united in the awareness of their duty to put their personal feelings aside in the interests of the client. George Steer writes: 'The more percep-tive, which included those who had tutor training, were able to see that these difficulties arose not from the encyclical, but from a complete misunderstanding of counselling. The need for fur-ther training of counsellors became all too evident and led to the formation of the tutor body. What started as a crisis in the CMAC became providentially a point of growth, introducing wider concepts of counselling. I see the conference following *Humanae Vitae* as a turning point in the CMAC.'[11]

Those who came confused and uncertain left greatly reas-sured. It was after all not a time for despondency but a time of opportunity. In the history of the CMAC Fr O'Leary's perfor-mance at the 1968 conference will undoubtedly go down as his 'finest hour'.

A Lasting Memorial

The most enduring legacy of the O'Leary years must be the place of the eucharist as the high point of the annual confer-ences. Nick Tyndall, as a guest from NMGC, remembers 'every-thing stopping for the Mass, with the long procession of white-robed priests signifying the essential difference between NMGC and CMAC.'[12] There were occasions when Mass was celebrated early in the morning to leave time free for the work of the day. Fr O'Leary and his conference organisers, among whom Dr John Marshall was a prime influence, placed the Mass as the centrepiece and developed the liturgy to express in prayer the bond in this pastoral work of the church, priests and people in the community of the eucharist.

The ceremonial celebration of the eucharist in this manner at the annual conference became a most unifying and uplifting experience, in a way that was difficult to convey to those back home, who had not been there. Now, of course, it has become the established practice at conferences and other occasions where counsellors are gathered together.

Looking Back

Canon O'Leary had great faith in the selection process and the training which he regarded as a necessary precondition for counselling in the CMAC. 'No one should do counselling unless they have been selected and trained as counsellors.' When asked in 1996 if he had any regrets or any views on the future of CMAC, he thought for a while: 'One of the things that comes back to me strongly is my failure to dispel the notion that the educational work was in some way second-class to counselling. The great aim was seen as marriage counselling. Many couldn't see that pre-marriage work and promoting the family was so important. Regarding the future, I think the organisation should not take itself for granted and indulge in navel-gazing. There is so much to be done, for example in the area of family research. The ideal is that the CMAC should be so effective that it is no longer needed! Now that is an ideal that will probably never be reached, but you do see what I mean!'

Of course he had his human side. It is evident that in the later years there were tensions between himself and the NEC. He had become a victim of his own dedication to the CMAC as his 'parish', in John Marshall's terms; as is the manner of the parish priest, he assumed complete control. (M 24) Inevitably there were problems. Marshall recounts the instance of the engagement of the prestigious Cooper Lybrand Associates Ltd, at the end of 1973, to carry out a management study of CMAC. Critical to such a study is the 'brief' or terms of reference given to the consultant and therefore a matter exclusively for the NEC as the 'employer'. But the NEC were not consulted! (M 36-7) With characteristic delicacy, Marshall does not say who supplied the terms of reference. The only reasonable conclusion is that it was Fr O'Leary himself – sublimely indifferent to the fact that his own performance as director would come into the ambit of the study! It might be added that another common attribute of the parish priest is not to perceive himself accountable to anybody other than his bishop!

In Memoriam

Canon O'Leary died on 31 August 1997. Of the many tributes paid to his memory, this reaction of his friend Monsignor Denis O'Callaghan to the news of his death reflects the depth of affection and regard he had won for himself in Ireland:

'I can still picture Fr Maurice with that familiar gesture of adjusting the wee skull-cap as he claimed that, of course, the truth must be compassionate! He had an extraordinary pastoral insight and a gift for getting the priorities right, opening up avenues of gospel promise when others were taking to the high moral ground ...

'What a host he was! A prince in his house. I can still picture him at the door of the CMAC in Lansdowne Road welcoming what he called the wild Irish – but he was Irish in heart and spirit, if a quieter mien. When I arrived he would call his dog Punch with the comment that here was someone who would walk him.

'CMAC and Fr Maurice have left happy memories. May the Lord give him that special place in the kingdom preserved for those who have discerned his will.'[13]

The Family Research Trust, which Fr O'Leary founded from the gifts received on the celebration of his thirty years as priest, remains as a testimony to his total commitment to the welfare of marriage and family.

CHAPTER 5

Early Years
A team of many talents

A feature of the CMAC in the foundation years was the remarkable array of talent it attracted from all walks of life in the Catholic community.

The Galaxy at Headquarters

Those of us from Ireland attending the annual conferences in England were impressed by the array of talent which Fr O'Leary had gathered round him. From the beginning, the CMAC attracted high calibre recruits from many professions including medicine, law and the army. Fr O'Leary continued in this tradition, following Cardinal Griffin's opinion that successful Catholic professionals were the best prospect for a lay apostolate. Fr O'Leary introduced graduates to the permanent staff and surrounded himself with a corps of dedicated high grade helpers, lawyers (including two judges) doctors, sociologists, communications experts and administrators, including at least one senior civil servant. When he set up a committee to get the finances in order, he had the services of highly qualified accountants under the chairmanship of the financial controller of Beechams! (M 40) Because he presided at every selection conference he had, of course, a unique knowledge of any exceptional talent coming into the organisation.

Twin Pillars

Pre-eminent amongst this galaxy were two doctors who were for many years the twin pillars of the CMAC. They were Dr (later Professor) John Marshall, a neurologist, and Dr Jack Dominian, a psychiatrist. Both went on to achieve distinction in their separate professions. They shared an enthusiasm for the CMAC and were the main thrust behind the training programmes and the creation of a tutor body. Together they raised the CMAC into a counselling service of professional standing.

They obviously also shared a deep well-informed faith and a commitment to the church and were involved in the development of an appropriate liturgy for celebration of the eucharist at conferences. Professor Marshall, who was a member of the Papal Commission on Birth Control,[1] is credited with introducing the church's *Morning and Evening Prayer*, based on the Divine Office, by which counsellors could take part in the constant recitation of those prayers throughout the world.

Their personalities were complementary. Marshall was the clinician, precise, methodical, effective, patriarchal, caring, shy of the limelight; Dominian the gifted communicator – verbally or through writing, high profile, controversial, authoritative TV panellist, prolific writer and brilliant lecturer.

Professional Authority

Professor Marshall's unique professional contribution was the establishment in the medical world of the validity of natural methods of family planning. Bernard Cawley says, 'recognising the inadequacies of the Ogino/Knaus, or "calendar" method of fertility control, he researched and promoted the "Basal Body Temperature" method. Before its publication he submitted his paper to the medical journals for professional scrutiny and assessment. His work, thus accredited, was largely responsible for the acceptance of the validity of natural methods of family planning in the secular world.'[2] Professor Marshall himself adds to this: 'The Family Planning Association were extremely strong and were dismissive of these (natural) methods. The CMAC met this by two ways, first of all by doing some very good basic research to establish its reliability and secondly, by insisting on it being taught by professionals. The reason why CMAC did this was firmly a matter of policy. Once the battle with the FPA was won and they began to accept its validity, the change (to teaching by counsellors) was made.'

Professor Marshall, the all-rounder, wrote and published *Preparing for Marriage*, which became the standard work on marriage preparation. Bernard Cawley again: 'For more than thirty years he conducted a correspondence service of fertility advice for women who were unable or unwilling to seek such help at CMAC centres. He was chairman of the Executive Committee responsible for the implementation of a management consultant report on the organisation in 1975 when the Irish CMAC became an independent body.' Relentless in the pursuit of excellence, he used his influence and administrative abilities in the creation of a structure that would provide a process of ongoing counsellor training. Broadly it consisted of a tutor body with access to the latest developments through specialists or 'consultants', and who would in turn convey these advances to the counsellors in the field. In this way the organisation would self-generate and self-maintain the highest standards.

Professor Marshall joined CMAC in 1951, in Fr Gorman's time, and quickly became a father figure in the organisation, a steadying hand at the wheel in times of domestic storms. He helped to build the CMAC from small beginnings through the years of expansion and change until his retirement 42 years later in 1993, an extraordinary record of unstinting service at the highest level.

Insights into Marriage

Dr Jack Dominian came in to CMAC in 1958. Few of us who knew him in those early years realised that this man would make such a contribution to the understanding of marriage in our lifetime. It began with the CMAC. 'Jack Dominian's experience as a marriage counsellor in the late 1950s ... caused him to rethink his whole understanding of marriage and marital breakdown.'[3] From that time his insights, as they developed, were disclosed in many lectures on marriage and family and have appeared in a veritable library of pamphlets and books.[4]

Dominian recognised the significance of the change in marriage from the old-time marriage based on duty to each other, to modern marriage, dependent on the mutual satisfaction of emotional and physical needs and, within it, the place of sexual intercourse as unifying force. (He found Humanae Vitae defective in its failure to fully recognise the function of sexual intercourse as a critical unifying element in marriage.) A most memorable contribution was his theory of marriage as a two-act drama, the first act as childhood with its needs of love and affirmation and the second act as marriage, with the same needs but providing a 'second chance' to heal the wounds and make good the deficiencies of the first. This view of marriage as an opportunity to heal, to affirm, to sustain, to support, to build each other, remains his most positive and encouraging contribution. For the believer, there is the added dimension of finding Christ in each other, and of the expression of their love, including sexual love, as the experience of God in their lives.

Conversely, there is the utter tragedy of failure. Dominian has devoted his life to the study of the conditions for the success of the marriage and those that lead to breakdown. He is one of the foremost living experts on the causes of marriage breakdown which he believes to be the most serious social evil in western society.

Dominian arrived in the CMAC in time to be a major influence in training all through its growth years. In Bernard Cawley's words: 'He introduced psychiatric insights into the counselling process whilst being careful to distinguish the counsellor's role from that of his own professional speciality.' His most important contribution was to provide an intelligible framework of reference for all those engaged in marriage counselling or in the preparation of pre-marriage courses (not to mention a better understanding of the counsellors' experiences in their own marriages).

After 36 years in CMAC, Dr Dominian, referring to the incidence of divorce, has come to realise that 'effective as counselling can be in individual cases, it is a totally inadequate response to the crisis that has arisen'.[5] He retains his belief in the CMAC's potential value; and 'still counsels couples with marital problems ...'[6]

Canon O'Leary pays fulsome tribute to the work of Drs Marshall and Dominian: 'They made a wonderful contribution at the time, particularly in the way of broadening the minds of the counsellors and particularly of the tutors.'

Well met in Ireland
Both Dr Marshall and Dr Dominian became well known to the Irish CMAC for their work in Ireland. Dr Marshall spoke at information meetings including those that preceded the setting up

of the first Irish centre in Belfast. Dr Dominian was a speaker at Irish conferences in the early years. Fr O'Leary was best known from presiding at selection conferences and helping with the basic training. He usually came with two helpers. Fr Frank Handley was one and, at the first selection in Belfast, the other was Mrs Monica Girouard. After that, it was the Irish born Mrs Fionnuala Arthur. These three became well known to that first generation of Irish counsellors. Fionnuala Arthur did one-to-one interviews at selections and was a tutor in counselling at the basic training (she was one of the first tutors in CMAC and trained by Jack Dominian). Warm and sincere, she was sensitive to the cultural differences: 'We so enjoyed the trips to Ireland. But it was different selecting there. The Irish were so warm, at ease, that you had to get beyond the comfortable exchange to find the insights and resources. With the English, their reserve often hid their warmth and understanding for counselling.'

Fr Frank Handley, small, dark, and alert, was a priest of the Salford diocese who was then head of training in London. He was kindly and perceptive and had a whimsical sense of humour. As the observer in 'group' at selections, his style was to put a question to the group and not to further intervene. The result was, much to his amusement, a reputation for being a bit dumb. He liked to tell of the Irish lady who, at the end of the selection day, remarked to her friend, 'that wee priest looks awful stupid, he seems to know nothing about anything'! Being so far off the mark about himself would not have lost her any credits from Frank if she had the other qualities he thought were needed!

Married Couples

London in those early years was remarkable for the number of married couples attached to headquarters. Among those who contributed to the first Irish conferences were Bob Townsin, a marine architect from Newcastle, and his wife Sheila. The doctors, Merlin and Patricia Marshall, were also from Newcastle. Quentin and Irene de la Bedoyere, experts in communication, came from London as did the experts in counselling practice, Tony and Rina Howard, who conducted the training of the first six Irish tutors to be trained in Ireland. Also well known to the Irish were George and Peggy Steer of the London centre,

Margaret Grimer who wrote books on relationships education,
Bert McConville (a Scotsman) later head of training in Dublin,
Bernard Cawley who, in 1982, was to be the first lay Chief
Executive since Graham Graham-Green, and numerous others.
Diverse as they were in terms of their skills and specialisms,
they shared without exception those qualities that made in-
volvement in the CMAC so satisfying: qualities of personal com-
mitment and generosity and of genuine friendship and caring.

Professor John Marshall CBE, KCSG, KSG. KSS,
MD, DSc., FRCP (Lond), FRCP(Edin), DPM
Emeritus Professor of Neurology, University of London.

Professor Marshall was born 16 April 1922 in Bolton, Lancashire,
and educated by the Salesians of St John Bosco. He graduated MB
BCh at the University of Manchester in 1946 and MD in 1951 and
Doctor of Science in 1981.

In 1954 he was appointed Senior Lecturer in Neurology,
University of Edinburgh and in 1956 Reader in Neurology,
University of London. He was appointed Professor of Neurology,
University of London, in 1971 and Emeritus Professor in 1987.

His involvement with the CMAC began in 1951 when he was
recruited by Fr Gorman to help with psychosexual problems.
Later he became involved in teaching and researching natural
family planning. This led to a number of scientific papers and two
books, *The Infertile Period* and *Planning for a Family.*

In 1962 Professor Marshal was awarded the KSS. In 1964 he was
appointed to the Papal Commission on Birth Control and in that
year also was awarded the KSG. In 1985 he was awarded the
KCSG. In 1994 he was appointed a member of the Warnock
Committee on Embryo Experimentation.

Professor Marshall retired from the CMAC in 1993.

CHAPTER 6

The Irish Connection
through English eyes

Professor John Marshall

An Englishman's view of the impact of the Irish on the English CMAC. (Marshall's Fifty Years of Marriage Care, *Chapter 13.)*

In making her progress report to the Executive Committee in January 1947, a bare five months after the opening of the London centre, the chief consultant, Mrs Graham-Green, provided a breakdown of the dioceses from which the applicants had come; one was from Ireland. What would make someone from Ireland with a marriage problem cross the water to England for help? To answer this we must go back to 1937 when Eamon De Valera was drawing up the constitution for the new Republic of Ireland. Unlike his forebears who had emigrated to the United States of America and embraced complete separation between church and state, he drew up a constitution for a Catholic state; the law of the Roman Catholic Church in the field of marriage and the family was to be the law of the land.

This meant no provision for divorce. So loud was the voice of the church against divorce, those drafting the constitution forgot that the church does in fact dissolve valid sacramental marriages on the grounds of non-consummation and provides for the dissolution of non-sacramental marriages, as in the Pauline privilege. So, couples whose marriage had been dissolved by the church could not be declared divorced by the state. They were free to contract a second marriage in church but in so doing they were open to a charge of bigamy by the state. The solution was to go to England to seek a divorce. Article 41 of the constitution forbade remarriage of persons divorced elsewhere but this seems to have been largely ignored. Thus began a trickle of applicants. This trickle was swollen by another group – those seeking a declaration of nullity from the church – because, in at least one diocese in Ireland, applicants were told such things were unheard of. They escaped from the consequences of this injustice by going to England; the marriage tribunals of the archdioceses of Birmingham, Southwark and Westminster became very familiar with these cases. But the first port of call for many of the people from Ireland in this situation was the CMAC in London.

The mandate of CMAC was limited to the United Kingdom which included Northern Ireland. In 1947 the chairman wrote to the Archbishop of Armagh offering help with establishing a centre in Northern Ireland; the archbishop replied that he saw no need for a branch of CMAC in Northern Ireland but would consult the bishops; nothing more was heard. The next initiative came from the Guild of Catholic Doctors in Belfast who, in 1956, invited Fr O'Leary to address them. They were concerned about the needs of married couples and had been pressing for some action. As a result of Fr O'Leary's visit, a further meeting of doctors, clergy and other interested people was organised in 1957 by the Newman Association in Belfast at which Dr John Marshall spoke. There was no immediate response by the ecclesiastical authorities; what went on behind the scenes is not recorded; among those who kept up the pressure for something to be done was Dr Raymond Magill. The result was that in 1962 Bishop Daniel Mageean opened the first centre in Ireland in Belfast with Fr Shaun McClafferty as priest chairman.

The first selection conference prior to this was a memorable experience; the plethora of talent, and the ease with which it had been assembled by the clergy, was in marked contrast to many areas in England where it was often difficult to muster enough candidates for a viable selection conference. Over forty candidates had been assembled, their ages ranging from 27 to 72 years. The twenty-seven-year-old was Sheila Campbell who, despite being below the age range for counsellors, was selected and went on to become a counsellor, a tutor and ultimately to run the service for teachers in CMAC Ireland.

The opening of the centre in Belfast had an immediate effect south of the border where bishops quickly invited Fr O'Leary to help with setting up centres. These followed in Limerick, Kilkenny and Cork in 1964 , selection and training being carried out by a team from CMAC headquarters in London with the help of Irish priests and others. Dublin already had a well developed pre-marriage education programme but no remedial counselling service; this followed in 1968 when a centre in Westland Row (later in Harcourt Street)[1] was opened, the priest chairman being Fr Michael Browne.

First mention of the need of the Irish centres to work towards independence had been made by Fr O'Leary in 1965. In 1966, Fr Michael Browne had been sent by the Archbishop of Dublin to CMAC headquarters at Lansdowne Road for two weeks to study the working of the organisation. In June 1969, the Irish centres held their first conference at Gormanston and decided to set up an ad hoc committee with two representatives from each of the four provinces and Tony Campbell from Newry as the first chairman. This led to the first National Conference, billed as such, being held in June 1970 which a number of people from headquarters in London attended. By this time there were eleven centres in operation in Ireland with nine more in the pipeline; the Irish tutors, who had trained with their English and Scottish colleagues at Pinner, were now undertaking most of the training of counsellors in the initial training courses.

In the Autumn of 1971, Fr Andy Kennedy was sent by the Irish bishops[2] to headquarters in London to study CMAC with a view to becoming the first Director of CMAC Ireland, and in 1972 the now formally established executive committee in Ireland began to send an observer to the meetings of the executive committee in London, Fr Michael Browne being the first of these. However, there was still considerable dependence on London, not only for the training of tutors. In 1972, Bishop Lucey of Cork closed the CMAC centre in the city because a CMAC doctor at a public meeting had given figures for the percentage of clients seeking help with family planning; the bishop regarded this as a breach of confidentiality. He insisted that the doctor issue a public apology or the centre closed; the doctor refused to apologise and the centre was closed. It took all of Fr O'Leary's considerable diplomatic skills to secure the opening of a new centre in the city to which some of the existing CMAC personnel were able to transfer.

Dependence gradually became less and, on 6 November 1975, the feast of All the Saints of Ireland, Fr Andy Kennedy became the first Director of CMAC in Ireland, thus ending the formal link between the CMAC centres in Ireland and headquarters in London. During his time at headquarters in London, Fr Kennedy had made a significant contribution, including acting as training officer for two years following the departure of Fr Handley in 1973.

The growth of CMAC in Ireland was truly remarkable. Between 1962, when the first centre was opened in Belfast, and 1975, when Fr Kennedy became the first director in Ireland, no less than 40[3] of the 56 centres in Ireland were established with the help of CMAC headquarters in London. This is all the more remarkable when it is remembered that Ireland was a separate country with a separate hierarchy, not to mention the significant cultural differences which existed. The success of the venture owed much to the skills of Fr O'Leary who won the confidence of bishops and clergy.

Formal separation of the two organisations did not end their relationship. Tutors from the two countries continued to train together and conferences in each country were always attended by representatives from the other, to the benefit of both. More important was the common bond of being eucharistic communities engaged in non-directive counselling of people with marriage difficulties in a Christian context. This unity of purpose survived the formal constitutional separation.

Dr Jack Dominian MBE, FRCPE, FRCPSYCH, DSC (Hons)

Dr Dominian was born in Athens, 25 August 1929, of Armenian father and Greek mother. At the outbreak of war the family fled to Bombay where he learned English, and in 1945 the family moved to Stamford where he completed his secondary education. He studied medicine in Cambridge where he met his future wife, Edith Smith, when they were both members of the Union of Catholic Students. In 1955 he qualified as a doctor and went on to do post-graduate studies in neurology and obstetrics. He obtained his FRCP in 1958 in Edinburgh.

In 1960 Dr Dominian began psychiatric studies at the Institute of Psychiatry, Maudsley Hospital, London where he received the Diploma in Psychological Medicine.

Dr Dominian joined CMAC in 1958. In 1971 he founded the Marriage Research Centre in London which, in 1991, was reformed and renamed 'One Plus One'. For his work on marriage Dr Dominian was awarded the MBE in 1994.

CHAPTER 7

The Irish Connection
through Irish eyes

Two Cultures – One Faith

Another Country

The Irish enjoyed their visits to England. There was an immediate bond in having so much in common with their English contemporaries: the selection and basic training, the approach to counselling and shared values as members of the same faith. There was also a sense of privilege in being part of this extended family in the church, part of a group which included so many gifted and generous people. And yet there was also a sense of separateness, of being different, as guests of a family who had grown up in another environment, sharing a different history and subtly different social values and meanings.

The English laity seemed more assured, more ready to assume leadership. This was in keeping with their status under their CMAC Constitution which vests ultimate control in the lay National Executive Committee which appoints the Chief Executive. The decisions of the English NEC do not require any further approval, in contrast to Ireland (where the Constitution, adopted in 1981, vests ultimate authority in the Episcopal Conference which also appoints the National Director).

The Pragmatic English

The English hierarchy took a more pragmatic view of the exercise of their authority. As an officially approved organisation within the church, the CMAC had to manifestly conduct its affairs in accordance with church teaching. In England, as in Ireland, there were no shortage of what Marshall calls 'the sniffers out of errors' (M 97) to alert the bishops to the slightest hint of deviation!

Marshall tells of an incident when an article in the *Daily Telegraph* grossly distorted the contents of a booklet written in co-operation with the Westminster Religious Education Council (WREC), a diocesan body, so as to imply that the CMAC was condoning, even encouraging, certain sexual practices. Cardinal Hume, Archbishop of Westminster and President of the CMAC, and in ultimate control of WREC, ordered the booklet to be re-written. When the Cardinal became aware that, by mistake, the CMAC had not been told in advance of the re-writing instruction he realised how much harm this could do to the organisation, and generously visited the CMAC headquarters on a healing mission. (M 48/9) The incident served to show that, in a church sponsored organisation, the hierarchy have sufficient power to intervene when they deem it necessary without having their authority written into a constitution.

The Clerical Role In England
When Cardinal Griffin, in 1951, appointed a priest to replace Graham-Green as chairman it was a strategic move, long advocated by Graham-Green himself, to win the confidence of clergy outside London. There may have been other factors at work but a desire to impose clerical control was not one of them. The fact that Fr Gorman had five selected 'placemen' appointed to the executive committee was evidence of his acceptance that the executive was the controlling body.

Fr Gorman was succeeded in turn by Fr Maurice O'Leary, Fr Ben Chalmers and Fr Peter Rudman – 31 successive years of priestly guidance. In 1982, however, the bishops of England and Wales found themselves unable to provide priests to work full-time in national lay organisations. Clearly the post, now designated chief executive, could not be filled on a part-time basis. The executive committee accordingly decided to appoint a lay person. The minutes of their meeting of July 1982 record their sensitivity to the issues involved. 'The National Pastoral Congress had urged the greater involvement of the laity in the church and there were many who would consider it right that a lay person should head the CMAC', and the counter view, 'It was true that some people inside and outside CMAC might be unhappy about the appointment of a lay person.' A subcommittee appointed to consider the implications concluded that, 'in practice it was possible for a lay person to be the chief executive but there would be need for a 'priestly presence' at the top, a priest as priest, not as a priest fulfilling another executive function.'[1] The first lay chief executive was Bernard Cawley, who served two contracted periods from 1982 to 1987 when he was succeeded by Jean Judge who in turn was succeeded in 1993 by Mary Corbett.

Class Distinction
In the 1960s, when the Irish first joined the English CMAC, they were interested to find, in discussion groups, that some of their English colleagues were concerned about the CMAC's perceived upper-class image, seeing this as a disadvantage. Such considerations would not arise in Ireland. The early records show that the foundation and establishment of the CMAC in England owed much to the support of upper-class Catholics. George Steer pays tribute to these people for their valuable work in those years: 'It was certainly from the support of upper-class Catholics that the CMAC grew and later flourished. I think the word 'quality' best describes them in that it acknowledges their social status, but more importantly, it recognises the overall quality of the person. The influence of such 'quality' persons continued and there were more than a few around when I joined the CMAC. As I saw it they were the backbone of the organisation. At the beginning they were the only ones whereas, in our later time, they were a few among many.' Patrick Seccombe, who on retirement from the British Council in 1976 joined the CMAC staff as an administrator, saw this support of the CMAC 'by the socially elite' as evidence of 'how very class orientated the church was.'

The many who succeeded the 'socially elite' appeared to inherit their best qualities of leadership and authority. They acknowledged their strengths and accepted authority more easily than the Irish. For example, the Irish had difficulty with the title 'tutor'. Willing and manifestly able to do the work, they shied away from the appearance of flaunting such a title, which at that time could lose friends and invite scorn at home! This bashfulness disappeared later.

Exchange of Talent

Nevertheless, at conferences and training weekends the Irish made their presence felt by their contribution to group discussion and to the liturgy. In return for English speakers at Irish conferences, they brought Dr Denis O'Callaghan (whose paper 'The Evolving Theology of Marriage' given to the first residential annual conference in 1966 was especially memorable) and Dr Kevin McNamara to a doctors' conference, while Dr Enda McDonagh collaborated with Fr O'Leary in the presentation of an historic paper prior to the publication of the encyclical *Humanae Vitae*. (M 33) Fr Andy Kennedy succeeded Fr Frank Handley as Head of Training from 1973 until he left to take over as National Director in Ireland in 1975.

Memories

The Irish also contributed in their peculiar national style to the social events when perhaps the cultural difference was most evident. The English social evenings tended to be formal, well organised affairs, artists on the stage and audience in their seats, attentive and respectful. This was in contrast to the more spontaneous 'McCarthy's party – all join in' Irish approach. The Irish, on the whole, were more prone to late night revelry, seducing the susceptible to join them in the song and the crack while the more prudent slipped off with their hot-water bottles to get a decent night's sleep.

Yet the English are nothing if not tolerant. George Steer, the archetypal civilised Englishman, is generous in his comments on the Irish as they took their leave for the last time: 'The extra dimension you brought, the fraternity that developed and not least, your contributions to the social evenings … it was a great loss to us when the time came for you to move on and establish your own organisation in Ireland. Not that it was a complete loss because our close co-operation continued and you left a treasury of experience and memories behind.'

CHAPTER 8

The role of the doctors

The Catholic doctors saw at first hand the miseries arising from uncontrolled fertility and broken marriages. They formed an influential lobby in the church in Britain and in Ireland for the provision of a counselling service acceptable to Catholics.

The Prime Movers

In his address to the Irish Conference of the CMAC in 1988, Canon O'Leary tells of how, shortly after his appointment as Chairman of the CMAC in London in 1956, he received invitations from a group of doctors in Dublin[1] and, separately, in Belfast (members of The Guild of SS Luke, Cosmos and Damien) to come and tell them the aims and objectives of this new service to marriage and family in the English church. 'Remember,' he said, 'it was the doctors in Dublin and Belfast who were the prime movers. They really must be given credit for that.'[2] Professor John Marshall says 'It was continued pressure from the Catholic doctors in Belfast, especially Dr Raymond Magill, which forced ecclesiastical authorities to open the first Irish centre in that city in 1962.' (M 101) This was a repeat of the history in Britain. Professor Marshall recalls that in the early 1950s doctors in Scotland and in the Birmingham centre were pressing for the extension of the service. 'I think the reason was that most of them were general practitioners and therefore they were seeing at first hand the problems people were facing and the lack of any provision by the church. In those days the idea of sending them (Catholics) to a non-Catholic agency was absolutely anathema, and I think that's why they were leaders in the field.'[3]

At the first Irish selection in Belfast in June 1962, 14 counsellors were selected and no fewer than 27 doctors appointed to the centre (doctors were not then subjected to the selection process).

Obviously this pointed to a widespread concern amongst the Catholic doctors. A few of the founding fathers of the CMAC in Belfast quickly identified the doctor who took the lead in having a marriage counselling service provided for Catholics in Belfast: Dr Raymond B Magill MD, at the time of writing in his 80s, lean, craggy and alert, part botanist, part philosopher, who spends his days in retirement tending the magnificent grounds of his home a few miles east of Downpatrick.

Dr Magill is renowned for his forthright manner. He got straight to the point. 'For me, it began when I was a student.'[4] A near relative, a married woman, had health problems which made each pregnancy a dice with death. Yet the pregnancies followed regardless, some children born normally, many lost in miscarriages. In the end she died leaving a husband and young family. 'I mean, she should never have had her pregnancies. Obviously she should have been on birth control. At the time no doctor would have anything to do with birth control. Then I became a doctor and took a deep interest in the safe period. But the safe period was frowned on.'

The Dark Ages

There was a small Catholic study group in Belfast in the early 1940s composed of professional people with a chaplain. Dr Magill was invited to give them a talk on sex and marriage. However the chaplain warned him on no account to mention the safe period. '"What," I said, "if they ask me?" "If they ask the question I will bring the meeting to a close," he said.'

The group went on to arrange careers guidance talks to Catholic secondary schools, inviting members of the various professions to address the students. These talks were much in demand. Unfortunately the head of the Civil Service in the North, who gave a talk, was a Protestant. When Bishop Mageean heard that the group had a Protestant lecturing in a Catholic school he ordered the group to be closed down.

Some years later the Redemptorists were organising retreats for Catholic doctors in St Clements in Ardglass. 'At question time, I raised the subject of the safe period which created a lot of discussion. Some doctors had heard that the safe period was now tolerated. The outcome was an invitation to Fr O'Leary, Dr

Marshall and a psychiatrist (Dr Jack Dominian?) of the CMAC in London to come to Belfast. All stayed in my house ... slowly the thing started. Eventually the bishop gave his consent ... they started the marriage guidance ... I was mainly instrumental in that.'

The church's attitude then was the more babies the better. 'I have been in houses in the city with only two bedrooms, front and back. In the front room is the mother and father and a couple of children. In the small back room as many as 8 children sleeping together, boys and girls, the girls menstruating, the boys lying in the bed beside them. Then the bishop would baptise the tenth child. The whole thing was utterly barbarous.' Housing was at a premium; young marrieds lived with relatives which led to more overcrowding, or found rooms, often where children were not welcome. A pregnancy could mean notice to quit.

Social Changes
Over the centuries, Dr Magill reasoned, children were a security in old age so that generally the more babies born the better from the economic and social point of view. All this began to change in the early 1900s with better living conditions. It began to be an advantage to limit the family. 'Marie Stopes started the idea of birth control with her book *Married Love* in the 1920s, intended to relieve women of the drudgery of unwanted pregnancies. A Jesuit wrote the introduction to that book. But the whole medical profession was against it. They would have nothing to do with it. It was only in the 1940s and 50s that the doctors began to discuss the problem. So the medical profession cannot hold up their hands now and say that the Catholic Church was solely to blame.'

'In the 1960s many people believed that the coming encyclical would allow (artificial) birth control. I was secretary to the Guild of St Luke, Cosmos and Damien. A lot of doctors had left the Guild because of Dr Magill's 'Protestant ideas' about birth control! I went to Cardinal Conway (a close friend). The Cardinal considered birth control would not be allowed because the church had condemned it through the centuries. I said the only reason for birth control in the past was to avoid the conse-

quences of adultery or fornication. That is why the church condemned it. In marriage the question does not arise.'

Discreet Obedience

'Eventually the encyclical came through and forbade birth control. The *Belfast Telegraph* rang me for my views. I said "I support
the Pope entirely. We will loyally help the people to use the safe
period".' The Cardinal was surprised and asked him 'why your
support for the Pope now if you believe him wrong?' 'I said (*The
Charge of the Light Brigade* was a popular film at the time) "Look,
it's like *The Charge of the Light Brigade*. The daft general gave a
daft order but at least the men obeyed. It was better to obey a
daft order than start arguing with the general!" I am, and always
have been, a sincere Catholic. But I believe that the church will
one day look back on its attitude to birth control then as it now
does on the Galileo episode.'

The doctors saw at first hand the consequences of uncontrolled fertility, the increasing incidence of marriage breakdown
and the misery that it caused. But the culture of the time
amongst Catholics, and not least their clergy, was that a marriage problem had to do with the sacrament and was therefore a
matter for the priest. 1947 saw the birth of a marriage counselling service in Belfast by the NMGC (now *Relate*). However,
in those days, as a non-Catholic agency, it was considered to be
humanistic in its values and therefore out of bounds for practis-
ing Catholics.

Dr Magill and his colleagues became convinced that a CMAC
centre should be established in Belfast. His office in the Catholic
doctors' guild placed him in a position of special influence and
he kept up the pressure on the bishop. The doctors were not out
to challenge the church. Indeed, as members of a Catholic doctors' guild it is obvious that their approach to their profession
was very much informed by their faith and its teachings. They
wanted the church to extend its pastoral care in the area of marriage by setting up this organisation of doctors and laity ministering to one another or, in the words of *Humanae Vitae*, 'like
ministering to like'. Eventually they got a response in Dr
Mageean's consent to the provision of a Catholic marriage counselling service in the diocese.

Courage Rewarded

The CMAC's introduction to Ireland arose directly from the concern of the Irish doctors for families in hardship and from the courage of a few to question the orthodoxy of the day. Dr Magill was destined to be the pioneer whose efforts led to the founding of the first marriage counselling centre in the church, and he remained to help with medical problems in marriage including psychosexual problems. Meanwhile the doctors in Dublin maintained their interest, and were actively involved in the establishment of the first centre in the city in 1968. The main mover then was Dr Jim Barnes, (brother of Dr Joe who first invited Fr O'Leary to Ireland), who had the distinction of being the first head of the psychosexual service in CMAC Ireland, acting in that capacity as consultant to the medical panel.

Raymond B Magill, M.D. FRCP. (Lond.), FRCP. (Ire.)

Born Belfast 1915, Raymond Magill was educated at Clongowes Wood College and Queen's University Belfast, where he studied medicine. For many years he was consultant to the Mater Hospital in Belfast including the turbulent times when the Stormont government refused to admit the hospital to the Health Scheme or to give it any financial assistance. As secretary of the Guild of SS Luke, Cosmos and Damien in Belfast, Dr Magill persuaded Bishop Mageean to set up a marriage counselling service for the Catholic community – the first such in Ireland.

Married (his first wife died from MS after many years illness), he has five children and numerous grandchildren. In 1984, Dr Magill was awarded the Benemerenti Medal by the Pope for his services to the Mater Hospital.

CHAPTER 9

1962: The birth of the Belfast centre

The persistence of the doctors eventually overcame the misgivings of Bishop Mageean of Down and Connor when he consented to the founding of the Belfast centre in 1962, the first church sponsored marriage counselling centre in Ireland. It was founded as an independent diocesan centre which did not come within the CMAC structure until many years later.

Doctors Force the Issue

After a few mix-ups in Dublin in 1956 Canon O'Leary set off for Belfast. He records, 'Things were very different in Belfast, so organised.'[1] He was quickly made aware of Bishop Mageean's reputation for caution when a local priest warned him that the bishop would never give you a 'yes' or a 'no'. True to form, the bishop was non-committal and nothing happened for another five years. Fr O'Leary is philosophical about the five year breathing space: 'In fact it was probably the best thing that happened because ... we didn't really have a working model to offer at that time, but in those five years we acquired a good working model.'[2] The bishop's caution in the matter is understandable. What was proposed here was the creation of a group of lay people, including doctors and other professionals, who would operate with the authority of the church in a sensitive area of pastoral work and who might not be readily amenable to clerical control.

In the event it was pressure from the Catholic doctors in Belfast, led by the intrepid Dr Raymond B Magill, that forced his hand. They were insisting that the church should provide a marriage counselling agency to help Catholic couples. The doctors' main leverage was the existence in Belfast of a non-Catholic agency as the only resource for married people. The National Marriage Guidance Council, now *Relate*, was in operation in

Belfast from 1947. While the NMGC is, and always has been, strictly non-denominational (its counsellors are drawn from all denominations including Catholics), it was nevertheless regarded by the Catholic clergy of that time as suspect and unsafe for any of their flock seeking help, especially in an area where birth control was in question.

Director Appointed

Bishop Mageean eventually acceded, but he took great care that the organisation would be directly under his control. He appointed a priest in charge who was known in the centre as the 'Reverend Director' in whom was vested absolute authority in all centre business, including the centre finances. This first Reverend Director was Fr Shaun McClafferty, a curate in St Teresa's parish on the Glen Road in West Belfast, and the centre was named the 'Down and Connor Marriage Advisory Service'. The historic first step is recorded in Fr Shaun's centre diary: 'Appointed Director on Thursday 27th April 1961 by Most Rev Daniel Mageean.'

Progress was slow because the work was left entirely to Fr McClafferty, in addition to his fulltime duties as a curate. Fr McClafferty, who had probably never heard of marriage counselling, was now faced with the task of informing himself of the whole business: of founding a centre, getting funds, finding premises and, not least, obtaining the co-operation of his fellow priests in the diocese.

Initiation of the Reverend Director

Fr McClafferty certainly justified the trust of his bishop by taking the job seriously. His incursion into this new territory was a model of clerical discretion. He played a lone hand and kept his cards close to his chest. Tall, balding, reticent, with a somewhat grave disposition, he had nevertheless, as his friends knew, a wry sense of humour. (He became very popular at social evenings at English conferences for his salty Belfast stories, read, po-faced, from his 'Bumper Fun Book'.)

In the months following his appointment he proceeded to educate himself by attending conferences on family themes in Maynooth and England and one in Paris. The proceedings were new to him and sometimes not all that clear. He liked to tell of the occasion when he went to an English CMAC conference in one of the northern universities, York or Keel. Arriving late he could find no one to direct him in the sprawling complex. At last he found a hall packed with delegates attentive to a somewhat indistinct speaker on a distant rostrum. He found a seat at the back and tried to follow the proceedings as best he could until lunch. It was then he discovered he was at the wrong conference. This one was a gathering of morticians and embalmers!

Nevertheless, he made sufficient progress to produce, in October 1961, a 'marriage document' for the bishop and priests and various others, including the Secretary of the Northern Ireland Council of Social Services, G B Newe.[3] Mr Newe, a Catholic, was helpful and made contacts in the pursuit of a government grant.[4] Fr O'Leary also gave advice and help to organise the first selection conference and the initial training programme. Doctors were canvassed and priests asked to submit names for selection. Contact was maintained throughout with the Vicar General, Monsignor Mullalley, acting presumably on behalf of the bishop.

A New Bishop

Bishop Mageean died on 17 January 1962. He will be remembered in the history books for the heroic stand he took on many occasions on behalf of the Catholics of Belfast and the North. He is entitled to be remembered also as the first Irish bishop to found a marriage counselling service in the church. Dr William Philbin, who succeeded him, was evidently equally in favour and supportive of the proposed centre and certainly equally concerned to ensure that it came under strict clerical supervision. He appointed two canon lawyers, Dr R Fitzpatrick and Dr J Cunningham, to ensure that all counsellors should be well grounded in church doctrine. At the completion of basic training courses in the diocese, which were conducted by the CMAC, these canon lawyers added a few further sessions presumably to ensure that no false doctrines had been imparted.

The selection in Belfast took place on 23 and 24 June 1962 in Trench House. The selectors were Fr O'Leary, Fr Handley, Fr Murphy, Dr Cunningham, Dr Marshall, Mr O'Malley, Mrs

Girouard and Mrs Ryder. Counsellors selected were Sean Breslin, Patricia Kearns, Sheila Campbell, James Crummey, Moya Hinds, James Mageean, James C May, Mary McCann, Patricia McGuigan, Frankie Macnally,[5] Seamus O'Hara, Terence O'Keefe, Catherine Scott, and Isobel Stewart, a total of 14, in addition to a panel of 27 doctors, the Reverend Chairman and the two canon lawyers. Amongst the men selected was one lawyer, Seamus O'Hara, which is unusual since at that time lawyers and doctors were engaged as 'consultants' and not ordinarily submitted to the selection process.

On 30 September 1962, Bishop Philbin addressed the new centre personnel, stressing their duty to 'uphold the principles of natural law', their special responsibility as Catholics and the unique value of voluntary work. He later arranged for some funding. Remedial counselling started soon after this. On 12 January the new premises at 11 College Square North were opened with 'Bishop Philbin, Monsignor Mullalley, forty priests, Mr Brennan, chairman of NMGC, Councillor Kelso, and 250 guests. We had internal television and a cup of tea for all present.'[6] On 13 January a secretary and assistant were appointed. The first pre-marriage course on 13 February 1964 started with '15 couples here and six in St Paul's. 5 talks on successive Tuesdays.'[7] Ireland's first Catholic marriage counselling service was under way.

From the beginning there were tensions between the doctors, who met separately, and the canon lawyers with their emphasis on church teaching, implying that doctrine took precedence over therapy. (According to Dr Magill one of these priests never changed his view that any method of birth control, including the safe period, was intrinsically wrong.) The counsellors were apparently more compliant than the doctors. Possibly they discovered that the debate was irrelevant since it is the needs of the client that dictates the counselling process – needs that seldom include strictures on canon law! The doctors depended on referrals but there were so few that in a short time most of the doctors had faded off the scene.

An Independent Service
The Down and Connor Marriage Advisory Service, as the name

testifies, was founded as an independent diocesan service and, while it called on the CMAC to conduct selections and basic training, at the operational level it maintained a certain detachment from the mainstream organisation.[8] It was no secret that some senior clergy in the diocese had a problem with the idea of non-directive counselling which they regarded as being inimical to the role of the 'teaching church'. These reservations on the part of the clergy were not unique to the church in Down and Connor. Marshall recalls similar clerical attitudes in the early days of the CMAC in England: 'an interesting example of the reactive and protective mentality prevalent among Catholics at that time; there was not so much concern to help Catholics with marriage problems as there was to prevent them being exposed to false teaching.' (M 13)

Two other features distinguished the Belfast centre from other centres in Ireland: firstly, educational work in schools was precluded and, secondly, married couples could not be counsellors in the centre simultaneously. The educational work in schools and training centres, which was a feature of the centre activities in the first years, was abruptly brought to a stop by the Reverend Director, almost as soon as it became established, on the grounds that he had not the time to supervise it properly. The reason why married couples could not serve together is not recorded.

From the enactment of the Constitution of CMAC Ireland in 1981 these distinctions began to melt away and eventually disappeared. One distinction that will remain is the dedication of the counsellors over the years, especially through the 25 years of the Troubles when they never ceased to be available to their clients, frustrated only when bomb-scares upset their appointments. Throughout these years the pre-marriage courses also continued regardless.

CHAPTER 10

From Belfast to Dublin and beyond

In the 1960s the CMAC began to take hold in Ireland. New centres appeared, some born from existing pre-marriage courses. Counsellors unexpectedly found in their training and practice of counselling a rewarding vocation which enriched their own living, their marriages and their personal faith.

And Then There Were Nine

In the six years from the Belfast centre's foundation in 1962 there was a total of nine centres in Ireland. Six years later there were thirty-three.[1] After Belfast there came in 1964 what Canon O'Leary called 'the triplets', Cork,[2] Kilkenny (Ossory), and Limerick, the first three centres in the Republic. The new counsellors did part of their training together in Cahir. Newry followed in 1966, Waterford and Wexford in 1967 and Armagh and Dublin in 1968. However, Dublin was something of an exception as we shall see.

In common with most Irish centres, except Belfast, the initiative in each case was taken by the clergy. Bishop Brooks of Dromore, then on the teaching staff of St Colman's College at Violet Hill in Newry, recalls a diocesan study group in the 1960s where marriage came up as a subject for consideration. Some people, he thinks possibly from the Belfast centre, were invited to talk about the CMAC, obviously to good effect. Bishop Eugene O'Doherty readily agreed to set up a centre in Newry. Fr O'Leary came from London to preside at the selection together with Fr Frank Handley and Fionnuala Arthur in 1966.

More typical was the foundation of the Waterford centre in that it arose from ongoing pre-marriage courses. These were run by Fr Robert Arthur, who had taken over from the founder, Fr Jim Walsh of Ballybricken, and catered for a wide area. In the words of Liam Hogan, one of the original counsellors, Fr Arthur 'was acutely aware that the courses needed updating ... and persuaded Bishop Michael Russell to invite Fr Maurice O'Leary from CMAC headquarters to address a conference of diocesan priests. Subsequently, at their conferences, Bishop Russell discussed with some fellow bishops the increasing incidence of marital breakdown, particularly among the younger married couples, during the sixties. He decided to invite Canon O'Leary to set up a CMAC centre in Waterford City.' The outcome was a centre for Waterford followed by another in the same year, 1967, in Wexford under Bishop Herlihy. There were other such instances where pre-marriage courses led to a CMAC centre. Dublin was one.

One of the reasons why Dublin did not come on board until 12 years after Fr O'Leary's visit in 1956 was that the Catholic Social Welfare Bureau in Dublin ran pre-marriage courses from at least 1958 and also had a Marriage Counselling Section. In 1958 the Director of the CSWB, Monsignor Barrett, reported to Archbishop McQuaid that the Dominican Nuns in Cabra had agreed to provide accommodation for 'the establishment of the CSWB's fifth pre-marriage course'.[3] It was in fact the Director of the CSWB, Fr Peter Cunningham, who organised the first CMAC selection conference for Dublin in 1968. His successor as Director of CSWB, Fr Michael Browne (who had been with the Dublin group from their selection) became their Director and had 'a major formative influence on the development of the service'.[4] In 1966 Fr Browne had been sent by the Archbishop of Dublin to the CMAC headquarters at Landsdowne Road to study the working of the organisation there, which presumably led to the setting up of the Dublin centre in response to the archbishop's wishes.

The Impact on New Counsellors

The process of recruitment and selection was set out by Fr O'Leary and has remained largely unchanged to this day. To him the selection was the key to the ultimate quality of the counsellors and the counselling. His abiding concern at home and in Ireland was that the standard of selection should not be diluted. He personally presided at all selection conferences until Fr

Kennedy took over as Director at the end of 1975. Local priests nominated likely candidates between the ages of 28 and 45 who were then invited by the bishop to present themselves for selection. At the time, marriage counselling was virtually unknown in the Catholic community so that invitations to join this new service were frequently received with a degree of incredulity. The common reaction was 'No! I/we have enough marriage problems at home.' Some reassurance from the priest organiser, plus the demon curiosity, usually overcame the initial reservations. (It was a CMAC maxim then that only conscripts made good counsellors – volunteers were suspect!)

Peter Nugent, selected with his wife Maureen for Dublin in 1968 and later head of training with Accord, gives an account of their recruitment which mirrors the experience of many of us before and since. As parents of small children they had organised a home-based group of friends to study matters of faith and family. Fr Peter Cunningham, Director of the CSWB, who was organising the first selection conference in Dublin, asked to attend a meeting and invited the group to offer themselves for selection. Peter and Maureen declined. 'At that time none of us had more than a hazy idea about marriage counselling,' Peter recalls. 'The selection conference took place over two half-days – Saturday afternoon and Sunday afternoon. On the preceding Thursday, Fr Peter telephoned us at home to enquire if we were going. We reminded him that we had decided against, adding that it was very short notice to arrange baby-sitters for both days. He said he was short of numbers and the archbishop would not be pleased. He was very persuasive. We attended on the understanding that we were not seriously interested.

'Experience of the selection process so impressed both Maureen and myself that we were delighted to receive an invitation to train. We accepted, not that we intended to be marriage counsellors, but we were owed something for the hassle of getting baby-sitters and giving up our weekend. Also, it was a new venture and might be interesting. At the end of the training course, the debt would be paid and we could walk away free of guilt. So what went wrong?

'After twenty one years Maureen resigned (from CMAC), having in the meantime acquired a university degree, a post-graduate qualification and a fulltime job as a Social Worker in a Special School. After twenty eight years, I am still active – at least some people think so – having occupied a variety of posts and having been a tutor for twenty years.

'People find themselves on initial training courses for all sorts of reasons. We met a group of wonderful people, warm, open, funny, committed and concerned, and one special priest. In the course of time, the priest became Right Reverend Monsignor Browne, but he was known as Fr B or Michael, with great respect and even greater affection. Who could walk away from such a group?'

The selection process and the basic training which followed made a lasting impact on the trainees, especially in the area of self-awareness and sensitivity for the feelings of others, not to mention new insights into the dynamics of the married state. People blossomed in this totally novel learning (or as some would have it, 'unlearning') experience. Sharing with others in the same mode was for most an unexpected source of enrichment. Mary McKeogh, a young mother selected for Kilkenny in 1964, remembers the effect of those days: (Her husband, Dr Tadhg was a consultant psychiatrist to the centre.) 'It was wonderful for me. I found an identity for myself when I was almost fulltime at home with four young children. It did wonders for my personal and intellectual development – I have lovely warm memories of the people with whom I worked closely. It and they gave me feelings of self-worth and affection ...'

But it was the face-to-face encounter with people in trouble that proved impossible to walk away from. Most of the new counsellors were unprepared for the depth of the ongoing and self-destroying misery and pain in marriage breakdown. As married people themselves there was a scary element in the realisation that this could be the outcome of the same dreams and hopes which they too had shared. And then to find that just by genuinely listening and caring they could bring a measure of relief and help to restore the self-respect and self-confidence of the client. It was scary and yet there was a sense of privilege in finding the gift to minister. There was in those early days a constant searching for ways of being more effective. Counsellors worked closely with the professionals, especially psychiatrists. Peter

Nugent writes of the Dublin scene: 'Our relationship with the medical profession was facilitated significantly by the presence in our group of Dr Jim Barnes who was (and is) widely respected among his peers. It was a time of great searching and questioning.' The marriage preparation courses which the Dublin CMAC inherited, as in other centres at the time, evolved from the old style talks by experts to less didactic, more 'client-centred' courses delivered by the counsellors themselves.

There was no shortage of demand for remedial counselling in the urban areas. 'When the first centre opened in Dublin we were not short of clients. At times it appeared to us that every priest in the city had been saving up his hard cases pending our arrival.'[5] It was different in the rural areas where people were more reluctant to go for counselling. Mary McKeogh recalls words of encouragement from Fr Handley: 'Everybody tells me that the Irish people will never go to see a marriage counsellor. This may be true. I'd like to think the whole of Kilkenny was queuing up for interviews but this may not be so. The really busy counsellors may still be playing games at school. This generation may have to see to laying good foundations for the next.'[6]

In an Alien World

The obverse side was the prevailing antipathy to marriage counsellors (not confined to the CMAC) in the community and the misunderstanding of the nature of counselling. 'The impertinence of these interfering busybodies – middle-class do-gooders dictating to others how to conduct their marriages!' was a typical reaction. Counsellors soon learned the futility of arguing the point and that confidentiality, the first principle of counselling, was best served by avoiding any discussions of the subject outside of the centre.

At another level there was the problem of clerical misunderstanding of the functions of the CMAC and what counselling involved. Mary McKeogh recalls a priest from an adjacent parish inviting the new counsellors in the early 1960s 'to come and talk with parents but only on condition we wouldn't mention family planning or sex education'! Some years later a parish priest, founding a new centre, expressed the hope that a centre in the area would help him to stamp out an outbreak of wife-swapping in the parish. Even the much loved and much admired Bishop Peter Birch, renowned for his establishment of a diocesan social service, by which people of all ages and creeds got involved in practical ways of helping the needy, could not understand why the CMAC would not go out and visit the people in their homes to facilitate them. (It is an absolute rule in the CMAC, as in most counselling agencies, that the initiative must be taken by the client; never by the counsellor.) The equally renowned Sr Stanislaus Kennedy, who wrote a book about the Social Services Centre in Kilkenny, was of a like mind. She considered the rule much too restrictive in the context of Kilkenny society and its needs.[7] In these circumstances the Kilkenny centre withered on the vine for a time but was restored to full activity later.[8]

Bishop Daniel Mageean

Born on a small farm near Saintfield in Co Down and ordained in 1906, he succeeded Bishop, later Cardinal, MacRory as Bishop of Down and Connor in 1929. His life as a bishop was blighted by many trials arising in the main from the bigotry of the Stormont regime which, in 1938, he denounced 'as one long record of partisan and bigoted discrimination'.[1] He endured the riots of the 1930s when thousands of his flock had to flee their homes. Many of his people were amongst the 745 victims of the air-raids in 1941. He was again in the wars when, after the 1948 Health Act, the Stormont regime denied any degree of funding to the Mater hospital because it refused to give up its Catholic ethos. Bishop Mageean died on 17 January 1962

1. *Ireland Since the Famine*, F. S. L. Lyons, Fontana, London, 1990.

CHAPTER 11

Independence

In 1975 the London office staff decided that they could no longer service the Irish centres. The Irish bishops accepted a recommendation from the Irish National Executive Committee (an ad-hoc committee which acted as the Irish contact with London) to institute the CMAC in Ireland as a separate organisation under the Irish hierarchy whilst maintaining the link with London.

The Presentation to the Irish Bishops

On the 25 June 1975 Bishop John McCormack, secretary of the Irish hierarchy, wrote to Fr Michael Browne, chairman of the Irish National Executive Committee of CMAC Ireland (INE). He informed him that at the bishops' meeting that month they had approved the committee's proposal to establish the Irish CMAC as an independent body, and had appointed Fr Andy Kennedy (then head of training in London) National Director Designate. Fr Kennedy 'doubled' from London until he moved into office in Ireland on 6 November 1975, the feast of All Saints of Ireland.

The bishops were responding to a memorandum from the Irish National Executive in May 1975 – a comprehensive review of the CMAC in Ireland at the time, its origins, its present strength and the INE's proposals for the future.[1] The acceptance by the bishops of these proposals, based substantially on the English model, determined for better or worse the structure of the organisation in Ireland for years to come.

According to the memorandum there were then 30 centres in Ireland incorporating a total of 981 priests, counsellors, doctors, nurses and legal advisors, providing remedial, educational and medical counselling on a voluntary basis and serviced by the CMAC headquarters in London. The time had come for a change. 'It is now suggested that the Catholic Marriage

Advisory Council, at present incorporated in England and Wales, should be incorporated as a legal entity in Ireland. Such legal incorporation of the CMAC here would facilitate negotiations with government departments, Health Boards and other statutory bodies.' The emphasis on 'legal' (underlined in the memorandum) is significant in that there is an underlying assumption throughout the document of a continuing relationship with London. 'It was agreed (with London) that the future aim would be independence with interdependence, the essential objectives being common high standards of selection and training and constant striving for improved quality in all areas of counselling.'

The need for reorganisation arose from the rapid growth in the number of centres and the need to service them, the need to establish a national legal identity for purposes of dealing with government, and 'the plain fact that London is unable to cope with our requirements as well as their own.' The INE proposed that its function as a national committee should devolve to a democratically elected body, an assembly representative of all the centres which 'subject to the hierarchy will be the general policy making and governing body of the CMAC in this country.' The assembly would meet not less than once a year and elect an executive committee.

The yearly cost of local centres was estimated at £2,500 each and it was concluded that 'A national administrative office is now essential for the purpose of consolidation and continuing growth – initially it will cost £10,000 per annum.' Then, significantly in the same paragraph, 'as an essential corollary to the developments outlined above ... the Irish hierarchy will be requested to:

(a) appoint a fulltime national priest director who would be their representative on both the assembly and the executive committee and

(b) confirm their continuing financial support of local centres and the national administrative office.'

In retrospect there were two major flaws in these proposals. The first was the failure to clarify the line of command in the light of the appointment of the director by the hierarchy (and not by the executive committee as in England), and the second was the gross underestimate of the cost of the national office (and indeed the local centres) which misled bishops and government alike. Both, as we shall see, subsequently gave rise to a lot of misunderstanding and heartache.

Nevertheless, the die was cast. The proposals to the hierarchy were the outcome of much deliberation by the Irish National Executive and the culmination of its work over the six years of its existence. With the formation of the first assembly and the new formally elected NEC, the INE quietly withdrew from the scene. The committee, which was founded as an ad-hoc committee by the chairman-secretaries meeting in Athlone in 1969, had done remarkable and largely unrecognised work in establishing a national identity for the CMAC in Ireland, particularly through the Irish annual conferences. It had won the recognition of the Irish government and, finally, with the approval of the Irish bishops, established a separate administration for the CMAC in Ireland. It is fitting to have a look at its history.

Canon Maurice Plunket O'Leary

Canon O'Leary was born in Kilburn 20 July 1920, the fourth and youngest child of John Joseph O'Leary from Piltown, Co Kilkenny, and Margaret O'Brien, born in Dublin. From 1924 to 1929 he attended St Dominic's Convent, West Hampstead, and from 1929 to 1934, the Salesian College Battersea. From 1934 to 1937 he attended St Edmund's College, Ware. In 1937 he went to the Venerable English College in Rome. The war intervened and he returned to England to complete his education from 1940 to 1944, in the Jesuits' College, Stoneyhurst, where in his own words he was 'given hospitality in St Mary's Hall'.

Ordained in the Sacred Heart Church, Kilburn on 13 February 1944, he was curate at Isleworth, Middlesex, from 1944 to 1952, and at Our Lady of the Assumption and St Gregory, Warwick Street, London W1, from 1952 to 1957. On 13 February 1956 he was appointed Chairman of CMAC by Cardinal Griffin, a post he filled (later as Director) until 1974.

He was appointed Honorary Canon of Westminster by Cardinal Heenan on 13 February 1974 and PP of All Saints, Kenton, Middlesex, by Cardinal Hume in April 1975. In July 1984 he was appointed PP of Our Lady of Lourdes, Harpenden, and Chapter Canon in February 1990. Canon O'Leary retired as PP of Harpenden in August 1995. He died on 31 August 1997.

CHAPTER 12

The Irish National Executive

Formed in 1969 mainly to organise Irish annual conferences, the INE developed over the years into a quasi national executive. In its later years, under the chairmanship of Fr Michael Browne, it was preoccupied with reorganisation as an Irish entity, mainly for the purpose of qualifying for government grants.

A Committee is Born
It was Fr O'Leary who first introduced the idea of a link between the centres in Ireland. In a letter dated 5 April 1969 to Eithne Maguire of the Limerick centre, he refers to a conversation with Cardinal Conway at the opening of the basic training course for the Armagh centre in January 1969: 'I mentioned to him the desirability of the centres in Ireland being linked together in some way, as this could prove a source of strength for the work itself and could also command greater respect in relations with government and other bodies. The Cardinal said he would bring this up at the bishops' Low Week meeting ... There is always a danger in creating a framework – not only may it not fit existing needs, but it may hinder growth. I think it is important to aim at as simple and flexible a structure as possible. I know there have been some fears that the links with the CMAC outside Ireland may be weakened by such a development in Ireland. It would be a loss for all if this were to happen especially now that the Irish centres are growing in numbers and experience; but I do not see why this should happen. Whatever service may be asked for will always I trust be given from here (London).' Fr O'Leary was concerned that, as the Irish became responsible for selection and training, they might succumb to local pressures for a lowering of standards and bring in people not of the required calibre. There would be proposals to enlist non-selected people, particularly for education work. 'Our policy has been that this should not

happen as it could easily endanger the reputation and therefore the acceptability of the work, not only of that centre, but throughout the country.' He saw a strength in having someone like him from outside not susceptible to such local pressures, at least until the principles for maintaining standards were set in concrete.

Fr O'Leary suggested to Eithne Maguire that a meeting of centres' (there were then 9) chairmen and secretaries could provide a suitable linkage. This in fact is what happened. Sometime later in 1969, the centre chairmen (mostly priests) and secretaries met in Athlone where they appointed an ad hoc committee which survived, with various changes of personnel, until it was replaced by the National Executive Committee elected by the assembly on 10 May 1975. This committee eventually had a member from each of the four archdioceses with a representative each from the priests and doctors and, later, the tutors. It referred to itself as the Irish National Executive to distinguish itself from the National Executive Committee in London. In the final months of 1974, however, it assumed the title of the 'Irish National Executive Committee', which can be confusing so for clarity it will be referred to here as the INE.

The committee had the advantage of being small, dedicated and informal. Mary McKeogh of Kilkenny, the first secretary, has no recollection of minutes. The other members were Fr Andy Kennedy of Cashel, replaced in 1971 by Fr Frank Buckley, Cork; Tony Campbell of Newry and Paddy Maloney from Sutton, Dublin, a Department of Education official, who made a special contribution as a good administrator. Jim Meehan of Newry, who arrived later as the representative of the tutors, found the proceedings more formalised. Minutes were kept by the then secretary, Elizabeth Roddy of Galway, and a periodic Newsletter issued to the centres. Fr Browne was in the chair. Also on the INE by then were Dr Maeve Twomey of Carlow, an important contact with the medical profession; Peter Nugent of Dublin, who had replaced Mary McKeogh, Jim Hewison of Waterford (who was the only member to be elected by the assembly to the new executive), and Gavin Halpin, a company director from Drogheda, who produced the first draft constitution. Gavin Halpin, incidentally, discovered Clongowes (where his sons were students) as a conference centre, which was to be the established venue for many years.

Fr Michael Browne

Though inclined to keep in the background in the early years, the man who became increasingly influential in the INE was Fr, later Monsignor, Michael Browne, first Priest Director of the Dublin centre and chairman of the INE in the later years. He was destined to play a major role in the evolution of the Irish CMAC towards an independent organisation.

Fr Browne was blessed with a most attractive personality, always with a twinkle in the eye, warm, genuine, committed and very capable. He was immensely popular. People trusted him and, more importantly, as Canon O'Leary said, 'the bishops trusted him', especially his own bishop, Archbishop McQuaid. In those years when London was the Central Office Fr Browne became effectively the chief executive of CMAC Ireland, and might have been a candidate for National Director. However, he adamantly refused to be considered, claiming that he detested administration. The refusal was in character since throughout his life he studiously avoided the limelight and delegated front line work at every opportunity. In committee his style was to facilitate rather than to lead. His reluctance to take a more leading role may have been connected with a hearing problem which necessitated the wearing of a hearing aid. He had a way of directing the hearing aid towards a speaker, in an attitude of concentration so as not to miss anything, which earned him the reputation of being the best listener in the CMAC. Dr Jim Barnes paid him this memorable tribute: 'Nobody heard so much as this deaf man!'

In 1966, at the archbishop's request, Fr Browne spent some weeks in London studying the working of the English CMAC, and from 1972 he attended meetings of the executive committee in London as an observer. Meanwhile he was co-ordinating selections and basic training in Ireland to dovetail with the work of the London office, so that he became intimately conversant with the organisation in both countries. Obviously he was determined to keep Ireland in step. In this connection the INE set about the organisation of Irish annual residential conferences similar to those in England, the first of which was held in Gormanston in June 1970. Peter Nugent recalls driving with Fr Browne on a tour of inspection of various seminaries and colleges in the Dublin area to find a suitable conference venue. Fr Browne was attentive to detail and personally invited the speakers. Another response to developments in Britain was the strengthening of the tutor body when, on 25 January 1975, he organised a selection process for potential tutors from which six counsellors out of fifteen invited were selected to go for training.[1] The INE were for a time preoccupied with the possibility of founding a Family Research Trust, similar to that set up by the CMAC in London, to mark the silver jubilee of Fr O'Leary's ordination. Unfortunately time ran out and nothing came of it.

From the 1970s the INE affairs were being conducted from the Harcourt St office and the increasing agenda began to tell. In the final paragraphs of the memorandum to the bishops in May 1975 Fr Browne says: 'In the past two years the Dublin centre has carried an unusually heavy burden of office and administrative work in respect of the CMAC in Ireland.' In June 1975, having won the bishops' approval for the INE proposals and seen the first assembly elect their executive and a National Director appointed, Fr Browne declined all invitations to further involvement at that level. He turned his full attention to the increasing demands of the Dublin centres which had grown to five in number by the time he retired in 1982. He is remembered by all who knew him with extraordinary regard and affection.

Mgr Michael Browne

CHAPTER 13

The Government Grant

Because of the prevailing perception of the CMAC as a diocesan-based voluntary organisation the Irish bishops had reservations at first about approaching the government in the South for a grant towards a head-quarters office. There were also special difficulties deriving from the Republic's Constitution which did not arise in England, where a substantial government grant towards the CMAC central office was available from the beginning.

The First Payment

Newsletter No. 8, dated November 1975, records Fr Kennedy's first meeting as Director with the new NEC as 'a happy one from more than one aspect. He was able to announce to the executive that he had received a cheque for £10,000 from the Department of Health as a grant in aid.' In addition, according to the secretary's report for 1974/75, department officials had assured a deputation in May 1974 that, 'the various Regional Health Boards would be informed on the government attitude to our work and how we should be supported.'

This was the outcome of a submission by the INE to the government in the Republic on 27 February 1974 requesting financial aid from central government towards a national office and from the Health Boards to the CMAC centres. The minutes of the INE meeting on 19 January 1974 refer to a 1971 application for financial assistance, subsequent meetings of Fr Browne and department officials, and of a meeting of Fr Browne and Mary McKeogh with Archbishop Cunnane and Bishops Kavanagh and Russell, 'representing Episcopal Pastoral and Social Welfare Commissions, also in this matter'. These discussions led to the renewed application, comprehensive and professionally presented.

The Bishops' Concern

The application for central government grant and its comparatively successful outcome might look on the surface a relatively
unimportant event, but in fact there are elements in the episode
which reflect the prevailing attitude of the bishops, the INE and
the government to the CMAC. It was a church organisation providing a voluntary service. In the minds of the bishops, who
founded the service on a diocesan basis, it was just one more
church sponsored organisation, if somewhat novel and more
specialised, in which worthy people gave their services free –
like the St Vincent de Paul, the Altar Society, the Offertory
Promise, and numerous other groups in the traditional mould –
voluntary workers assisting the clergy in running the church.
The notion of state involvement did not sit easily in this church
domain and this was reflected in the circumspection of the INE
and the bishops in their approach to the government for a grant.

The precedent for government assistance to the CMAC was
well established in Britain and in Northern Ireland. The CMAC
in Britain had government assistance almost from the start, as
indeed had the Belfast (Down and Connor) centre (as a service
centre for the North) from the old Stormont government. In their
submission to the Irish government, the INE pointed out that, in
1973, the CMAC headquarters in London had received £30,000
from the exchequer and the Belfast centre £2,500, in addition to
£1,000 from Belfast Corporation and smaller amounts from
Antrim and Down County Councils. In both Britain and Northern
Ireland there were statutory provisions for such grants subject
only to periodic reviews to ensure specified conditions were
being met.

Special Problems in the Republic

In the Republic, however, things were not so straightforward.
Firstly the government in the Republic has to be careful dealing
with church-sponsored bodies as the 1937 Constitution pre-
cludes it from making 'any discrimination on the ground of religious profession, belief or status'. Secondly, unlike Britain, there
was at that time no provision for statutory payments from central government to voluntary bodies. There was of course statutory provision for payments from Health Boards to centres but

payments towards the cost of the central office were made at the Minister's discretion and obliquely through an appropriate Health Board. There was therefore no guarantee of such payments being continued and, more importantly, they had to be re-negotiated with each change of government.

In these circumstances, with so much of a 'grace and favour' element involved, the bishops and their negotiators had to be sensitive to the danger of political involvement or of opening the door to bureaucratic intrusion into church matters. In the run-up to the submission there was constant contact between the INE and bishops' representatives. Eventually a notice to the Irish chairmen and secretaries of 26 November 1973 announced that: 'The Hierarchy, through the Episcopal Commission on 16 November 1973 has given approval to the (Irish) National Executive CMAC to request the government
  (a) for financial assistance at national level and
  (b) to empower local authorities to give grants to
  local centres.'

The deputation appointed to meet the government were: Fr Browne (Chairman), Elizabeth Roddy (Secretary), Dr Brian Lemass, Dr Fahy (Psychiatrist), Bishop Kavanagh and Diarmuid Quirk. On reserve were Eithne Maguire and Bishop McCormack. Of all these, only two were members of the INE.

Basis of the Claim

Their case was based entirely on the service being provided in the area of marriage and family, the stability of which was vital to the well-being of society: 'Investment by the community of money, energy and time in sustaining and improving the quality of marriage and family life will thus be amply repaid.'

'The Catholic Marriage Advisory Council (CMAC) is a voluntary agency which aims at providing a comprehensive counselling service in the area of marriage and family life. Its members are carefully selected and trained for this work.'

The statistics are impressive. In 22 centres in the Republic and 3 in Northern Ireland, in the year ended 31 December 1973, a total of 696 trained personnel, marriage counsellors, doctors, psychiatrists, priests, nurses, and legal advisors, counselled 5,435 people . In that year 7,210 attended pre-marriage courses and 11,010 parents and 9,277 young people attended courses in personal relationships and sex education. The entire cost to date had been borne by the Irish bishops. The service was available to all without regard to religious affiliation.

A Foot in the Door

The cheque for £10,000 as the first of (implied) yearly payments, and perhaps more importantly, the positive instructions to the Health Boards in regard to the centres, made history as the first acknowledgement by the Irish state that the CMAC's input deserved recognition. But in the light of the huge input (and uptake) of services at a professional level, the response in money terms now looks derisory. There is no evidence, however, that anybody thought so at the time. The government could of course rightly say that its obligation was limited, in that prior approval was never sought or given for the provision of such a service. Yet the area of marriage and family was undeniably one of public concern. The emergence of a voluntary group with the scope and professionalism of the CMAC should have been recognised as a development worthy of substantial government support. Had the value of the service been calculated in true economic terms – that is what it would have cost the Health Boards to provide it themselves – the figure might have raised a few eyebrows. Not only was this not done but no mention whatsoever was made of the considerable capital expenditure involved in providing CMAC accommodation.

Capital Costs of Centres

A CMAC centre cannot be accommodated in a church hall or vacant classroom. It requires exclusive use of a building in a suitable location with a number of furnished rooms for counselling, one or more large rooms with seating for pre-marriage courses, an office equipped for a secretary, cloakrooms, washrooms, a heating unit, and all the facilities necessary where the public is admitted.

At a conservative estimate, such a unit in the commercial market would be valued, at that time, at not less than £50,000 which, for 22 centres represents £1 million capital, injected by the church into the Republic's social services. No recoupment was claimed, although there is an analogy in the government's grants towards the capital cost of schools provided by the church. The INE submission estimated the average running costs of a centre at a minimum of £2,300 per annum. However, Fr Kennedy, in a submission to the Episcopal Conference in February 1978, put the running costs 'in secular terms' in the region of £3,500 to £4,000 per annum. The amount of grant from Health Boards (where paid) varied, but was seldom more than one tenth of the running costs.[1] It must be said that some centres were less than efficient in the submission of claims.

The fact was that, at the time of the transition towards independence, the perception of the CMAC in the minds of the bishops and of the government was of a Catholic voluntary organisation, and therefore appropriately financed from church funds. Any offering from the public purse, while welcome as a courteous recognition of its contribution to the public good, was not expected to be more than peripheral.

Realism
In the following years the unexpectedly high cost of the central office brought about a change of attitude, yet sensitivity towards dependence on the government of the Republic lingered. Following a meeting of the standing committee of the Episcopal Conference, we find Fr Kennedy, National Director, writing on 4 October 1978 to ask permission to take certain steps enabling him to raise funds: 'This would open the way to fund raising from a variety of sources, and we would bear in mind the point regarding the danger of over-dependence on the state.' Bishop McCormack, Secretary to the Episcopal Conference, wrote to Fr Kennedy on 21 October 1978: 'In the present sensitive period, no approach be made to a Minister of State or civil servants on behalf of CMAC until a constitution has been approved.' However, in a letter of 12 December 1978, Bishop McCormack, on behalf of the Standing Committee, told Fr Kennedy that: 'It was agreed that you be authorised to approach the Department of Health, under the procedure laid down at the October 1978 meeting, along with Bishop O'Mahony, to seek a grant in aid for the remainder of 1978 and (for) 1979.' After 1980, when the Financial Controller's estimate of the cost of central office for the following year came to over £177,000, there is no further evidence of reservations about accepting government funds.

CHAPTER 14

Towards a New Constitution

From 1974 the INE had given special consideration to the drafting of a constitution which would incorporate the CMAC in Ireland as a legal entity. It was 1981 when a constitution acceptable to the Episcopal Conference was agreed.

First Perceptions

The work of the INE in its first years was almost exclusively the organising of the annual conferences. As the organisation expanded, the possibility of government grants came on the agenda. In pursuit of these, a degree of Irish autonomy was necessary to meet government requirements. The problem was how to achieve this without breaking the vital link with London. The maintenance of the link was the main concern of the committee when considering possible new structures. A formula by which this could be done was a feature of the proposals for Ireland put to the bishops and to the first assembly. In the event, the decision of the first assembly that a constitution was unnecessary, and the subsequent independent behaviour of the National Director and the Irish NEC, effectively severed the legal connection with the parent body in England

When the application for government grant was made in 1974, the CMAC was legally an English organisation. The executive committee in London had rules made in April 1968 under their Articles of Association to allow them to operate in Ireland. But normally only an Irish institution would be eligible for grant aid from the Irish government. The INE therefore turned its mind to constituting the CMAC in Ireland as a national entity. There was an additional motive in that Fr Browne was uneasy about the status of the INE, as an ad-hoc committee appointed by the chairmen and secretaries meetings, negotiating with the bishops' authority on behalf of the CMAC in Ireland. The whole question of a new constitution was precipitated into action in the closing months of 1974 and the spring of 1975.

Introduction of Democracy

Gavin Halpin of the INE was the main mover, assisted by Desmond Donovan BL, legal advisor to the INE. A Mr Matt O'Brien of Kilkenny is also mentioned in this connection. At the meeting of the INE on 14 December 1974, Gavin Halpin proposed that the committee should proceed forthwith to replace the chairman and secretaries group with a National Council, representative of all the centres, which would elect a National Executive with powers of co-option. The committee favoured the proposal and agreed to put it to the chairmen and secretaries meeting. In a circulated overview dated 30 December 1974, Fr Browne reported that the chairmen and secretaries meeting the previous January had mandated the INE to 'do something about a constitution. While not rushing the constitution aspect, we feel that there is urgent need to clarify ... the method by which the executive committee should be selected.' The immediate task was to devise a democratic system for this purpose and to clarify the new executive's mandate, its relationship to the Irish centres and its relationship to the NEC in England.

Early in January Gavin Halpin produced a working document in response, acknowledging that a constitution would entail prolonged negotiation with the English executive. In answer to Fr Browne's questions, he proposed a process by which a new executive could be put in place immediately. He proposed a National Council composed of centre representatives 'to be the governing and policy-making body of the CMAC in Ireland, North and South ... which would elect by democratic process a National Executive Committee, to implement its policy and carry out the day to day business of running the CMAC in Ireland.' He went on to detail the composition of the executive including a 'Priest Chairman or advisor – appointed by the hierarchy.'

The Legal Dimension

Gavin Halpin's proposals were reviewed by Desmond Donovan

in a memorandum dated 13 January 1975, a document remarkable for its legal insight and clarity of presentation. He opens: 'I have had correspondence and consultation with Gavin Halpin and I have found to my pleasure that our minds are *ad idem* in broad terms on the structure of the Council in Ireland.' Donovan is particular about terms: 'Council' means the whole body of the CMAC in Ireland; 'Centre', the basic unit of the Council, 'means a group of registered members of the Council formed for the purpose of promoting the objects of the Council and having a specified address.' Centres would nominate representatives (one or more depending on numbers) to an all-Ireland body for which he proposes the term 'assembly' (not 'conference' which had acquired another meaning as an annual event of recent years). 'The Irish Episcopal Conference shall be invited to appoint one member of the assembly.' The assembly would select from and by its members the personnel of an executive committee which should be termed the 'Ireland Committee' and which would consist of a 'Chairman, Secretary, Treasurer, Registrar, Spiritual Director and ordinary members'. The functions of the assembly are detailed in a way that leaves no doubt of its status as the governing and policy making body of the Council to which the Ireland Committee, charged with executing its policy, would report.

All this was essentially the moulding of Gavin Halpin's proposals into legal terms. But the core of Donovan's memorandum is his solution to the problem of achieving autonomy for the Irish CMAC while preserving the link with the parent body in London. By rules made in 1968, the CMAC in England provided for Irish centres to be included in their organisation and to describe themselves as CMAC centres. Donovan concludes that the CMAC, a limited company in England, could, by amending the rules (he preferred 'regulations') incorporate itself in Ireland with a registered office here. 'It is possible for the Council as incorporated in England and Wales to be incorporated in this country and if this were to be done the Council would have a registered office within this jurisdiction. The directors of the company registered in Ireland need not necessarily be the directors of the company registered in London.'

This was an ingenious plan for devolution which would give

virtually total autonomy to the CMAC in Ireland while remaining a constituent of the English organisation. Interestingly Donovan records in his memorandum that the then Secretary of the Department of Health, Mr Murray, stressed the importance of maintaining the link with the English CMAC, referring to 'the cross-fertilisation of ideas and the significance of the research into various aspects of social conditions and social welfare and matters of health originating in Britain.'

Adoption

Obviously the rules would have to be acceptable to the NEC in London and, equally obviously, to the bishops of Ireland. There is no evidence that the proposed amendment to the rules was ever submitted to either. On 18 February 1975 the INE produced a summation of the Halpin-Donovan papers as formal proposals for the consideration of the forthcoming annual conference at Clongowes, 4-6 April 1975, and later to the new assembly for adoption. These proposals had one new and vital element which did not arise from either Halpin or Donovan – the appointment of a National Director by the Irish hierarchy.

The memorandum incorporating the proposals, dated May 1975, was submitted to the Episcopal Conference for the bishops' approval. According to the memorandum the proposals had been 'endorsed' by the CMAC conference at Clongowes and were now being submitted to an assembly called for 10 May 1975. The bishops' approval, addressed to Fr Browne on 24 June 1975, made no comment on the proposals other than confirmation of Fr Kennedy's appointment as 'National Director Designate' and requests for further information on the financial implications of the new structure.

The First Assembly

Following the conference at Clongowes, the INE called a meeting of centre representatives which met in 35 Harcourt Street Dublin on 10 May 1975. In attendance were the INE: Fr Browne (chair), Elizabeth Roddy, Peter Nugent, Jim Meehan, Jim Hewison and Gavin Halpin (the last two doubled as centre members), and one representative each from 29 centres. Two of these (Fr Hilary Armstrong, Belfast and Fr Fred McSorley,

Downpatrick) were representatives of the Down and Connor Marriage Advisory Service and, as such, considered themselves at this stage 'associates' of the CMAC. As fraternal representatives they did not vote.

According to the minutes, Gavin Halpin explained the idea of an assembly and that the main purpose of this meeting was to elect a national executive (NEC) of six members. The meeting then resolved:

> *Director.* The Priest Director would be the CMAC's link with the hierarchy. It is generally thought that Fr Andy Kennedy would be the ideal man for the job and (it) was recommended that his name be put forward to the hierarchy. The assembly concurred with this.
>
> *Constitution.* No separate constitution is needed. A nominal company, CMAC Ireland, will need to be formed using the constitution of England. Powers will be given to assembly which in its turn will elect an executive. Our own emphasis can be put and our structure should be flexible. It is important that we keep a strong link with Britain and that we should be interdependent.'

After some further business the minutes record that, on the proposal of Matt O'Brien, seconded by Fr Donal Casey, the meeting constituted itself an assembly and elected six of those present to the NEC, the first formally constituted National Executive Committee of CMAC Ireland.

The CMAC Newsletter No. 7, dated June 1975, confirms the minutes of the assembly and clarifies somewhat the decision regarding the constitution. Note 5 reads: 'Consideration will be given to forming a nominal company for CMAC (Ireland) using the British Constitution which can be adapted to our needs. It is recognised as important that we maintain a strong link with Britain.'

It is evident that the assembly (a) saw Fr Kennedy in the role of bishops' representative on the executive rather than as the chief executive, and (b) saw no contradiction between the decision to have no constitution and the formation of a nominal company within the British CMAC Constitution. The assembly made no reference to the fact that the necessity for an Irish constitution first arose as a government condition for payment of

grants. In the event, the incoming NEC made no effort to implement this policy decision to form a nominal company, settling
for an inconclusive status quo.

Bishops' Concern
Eventually it was the bishops who took the initiative. Becoming
increasingly concerned at the growing prominence (and cost) of
the central office, they saw the necessity for a constitution to set
the boundaries. On 21 October 1978 Bishop McCormack as secretary of the Episcopal Conference wrote to Fr Kennedy from
the Conference: 'It was also agreed that the future development
of the CMAC in Ireland needs to be charted with care, taking
into account the resources of personnel and finance available to
us ... The urgent need for a constitution was once again acknowledged, but it was agreed that a constitution for CMAC in Ireland
must explicitly reflect and preserve the diocesan structure and
format, and at the same time provide for necessary service structures, maintaining a proper and reasonable balance between the
two aspects.' Fr Kennedy's reply on 25 November 1978 from the
working party was compliant to the letter: 'The working party[1]
has asked me to convey its appreciation of the comments of the
Episcopal Conference and to indicate its desire to maintain a
proper and reasonable balance between the two aspects of the
CMAC, namely the diocesan structure and format and the central services provision.'

Bishop McCormack wrote again on 12 December 1978, apparently in response to a draft submitted by the working party:
'A number of principles and guidelines and further suggestions
were made by the bishops' committee (Bishops Lennon, Cahal B
Daly, Casey and O'Mahony) ... It was felt that satisfactory
progress is being made and it was agreed that the bishops' committee and the drafting committee of CMAC should meet to discuss the final proposals and to discuss the various proposals and
hopefully to prepare the way for a final draft.' That proved to be
somewhat optimistic because it took another year and a half before the Bishops' Conference gave their conditional approval.
Obviously the bishops' committee found it very difficult to produce a draft acceptable to the twice yearly meetings of the full
Conference. It was not until 24 June 1980 that Bishop

McCormack could write to Fr Kennedy: 'At a meeting of the bishops this month the draft constitution of the Catholic Marriage Advisory Council of Ireland and a number of cognate matters were considered. It was decided that, subject to a number of amendments suggested during the course of the discussion, the draft Constitution be approved for a period of three years. It was also decided that the diocese should remain the basic unit of the CMAC.'

The End Product
The *Constitution of The Catholic Marriage Advisory Council of Ireland* (North and South) came into force on 1 February 1981[2] and has survived with some minor amendments to this day. It provides for an autonomous administration in Northern Ireland recognised by the government in the North as a separate entity. First conceived as a mere prescription to meet the needs of government for grant purposes, and to clarify the connection with the 'parent' body in London, it became a confirmation of ultimate clerical authority as the wording in Section 2, 'Aims', shows:

'CMAC is a voluntary, predominantly lay, organisation working in co-operation with and under the special direction of the Catholic hierarchy in Ireland, serving people primarily in the areas of marriage and family relationships. As a service agency of the dioceses and in accordance with the teachings of the church on marriage and family life, it aims to promote a better understanding of Christian marriage and to help people to initiate, sustain and enrich their marriages and family relationships.'

If the words 'and under the special direction of (the Catholic hierarchy)' were omitted from the above it would lose nothing whatever in terms of fulfilling the stated aims. But the document is notable for dependency at every stage on the approval of either the hierarchy or of the local bishop or both. Clause 6 (1), which defines the status of the assembly as the governing body, states emphatically that: 'Without prejudice to the authority of the Episcopal Conference and to the authority of each bishop within his diocese, the governing body of CMAC shall be the assembly.'

This section sought to establish the authority of the assembly while recognising the responsibilities of the bishops within their dioceses. The effect was to provide for a dual authority: the assembly on one hand and the Episcopal Conference on the other. However, when Fr Kennedy took up his appointment six years earlier as the first National Director, he elected to report directly to the bishops in the Episcopal Conference as their appointed executive officer and in the traditional manner of a priest being subject to the authority of his bishop. As a consequence the assembly and the NEC had been relegated to a secondary role whose decisions would be taken in collaboration with the National Director and would eventually be subject to the bishops' approval. In practice this continued after the constitution was introduced.

The constitution did, nevertheless, secure the authority of the organisation in the domestic and professional areas at national and local level and ensured that the whole area of quality control was vested in the organisation. The constitution also provided that the central office may, in consultation with the local bishop, withdraw recognition of membership from any person or from a centre in certain circumstances subject to specified safeguards.

By the time the constitution was enacted, whatever intention the original architects may have had to found a lay organisation answerable to a democratically elected assembly had disappeared. The laity were assigned to their age-old role as voluntary helpers to the clergy. There were no complaints. For both clergy and laity the needs of the clients were paramount and constitutional niceties took second place. Desmond Donovan's elegant measures for continuing contact with the parent body in England never surfaced again. The Irish constitution makes no reference whatever to its foundation in the CMAC in Britain.

CHAPTER 15

The Central Office

The institution of an Irish CMAC in 1975 coincided with an urgent need for more intensive training, requiring a corps of specialists at central office which, in terms of control and cost, was far beyond what the bishops had been led to expect.

Two Divergent Views

As we have seen from the laborious birth of the constitution, it was the establishment of the central office for Ireland which brought to the surface a serious divergence between the bishops' view of the organisation in Ireland and the view of Fr Kennedy, the National Director, based on his London experience. To understand how this divergence arose it is necessary to look at the background of the organisation in both countries.

The vital difference was that in England the CMAC began as a headquarters or national office out of which the centres grew like satellites, the first being the London centre in the days of Graham-Green. In Ireland it was the satellites, the centres, which appeared first, with the headquarters office well out of sight in London for many years. When the time came for a headquarters office in Ireland it presented some problems for the Irish bishops.

A Separate Tradition

The foundation of the English CMAC and its subsequent development at the institutional level was fundamentally different from the CMAC in Ireland as recent events show. In England the executive committee was, and remains, the controlling body and has had a healthy tendency, in recent years, to devolve more power to its chief executive officer and headquarters staff. Marshall gives an example during the period when Jean Judge was chief executive (1987-1993): 'The decision to recognise a new centre or to close an existing centre was no longer taken by the executive committee but by the chief executive, who then reported it to the executive committee ... This and other examples reflected the growing professionalism of the headquarters staff. Decisions on policy remained very much the province of the executive committee but the background papers and policy proposals were prepared by the headquarters staff for the committee.' (M 65)

The Charities Act of 1992 required the CMAC in England to clarify the legal relationship between the central executive committee and the centres. Marshall writes that it was decided that the centres' finances should be the responsibility of the centres. 'The executive committee would be responsible for selection and training and would lay down rules for the conduct of work in the centres. The sanction for failure to observe these rules would be withdrawal of the right of a centre to use the name CMAC. The centres were not, therefore, "branches" of CMAC Ltd; they were independent bodies using the name CMAC subject to approval by the executive committee.' (M 64)

A Revolution in Counselling Skills
It was Fr Kennedy's good fortune to be a member of the London headquarters staff from 1971 to 1975, a crucial period of growth and change in the administration of the CMAC counselling service leading up to independence in Ireland in 1975. The skills of counselling had come a long way from the first days in London when counsellors, known then as 'consultants', 'advised' the client, or, in short, practised 'directive counselling'. Very soon, however, under the influence of Carl Rogers, the perception of counselling changed towards a non-directive technique of enabling the clients to come to their own decisions. Attending and listening, and respect for the client as a person, became the key to the process. A Jesuit, Felix P Biestek, drew up rules for counselling based on the Rogerian principles which became a textbook for the CMAC. In the 1960s further insights were emerging in Britain and America from research institutes and from workers in the areas of psychotherapy, including the CMAC's own experts, doctors John Marshall and Jack Dominian.

A rising prophet of counselling in those days was a priest of Irish descent, Fr Gerard Egan of Loyola University in Chicago. His intensive training methods were to become the basis of CMAC training in Ireland and in Britain. Egan stressed the counsellor's professional responsibility to have the skills necessary to help the client, skills which must be learned and practised. Egan held that inefficient counselling was not only a sterile process but could actually be harmful to the client, the insidious element being that neither the client nor the (inadequate) counsellor would suspect this. This placed a heavy responsibility on those providing a counselling service to ensure that the counsellors were adequately trained.

As we have seen, the main preoccupation of the CMAC in England, after the 1968 conference in Spode, was the development of a training network which would effectively transmit these new insights and techniques to the counsellors in the field. From this emerged the 'tutor body', a corps of tutors throughout the country trained by specialist consultants and serviced by a support structure at headquarters which included graduates on the permanent staff. This was the model of a central office which Fr Kennedy brought to Ireland when he arrived as National Director at the end of 1975. However, it was very far removed from the model of the central office which the Irish bishops had in mind when they appointed him as the head of an independent Irish CMAC.

When he took office, Fr Kennedy was painfully aware that, except for the tutors, the Irish counsellors had little more than a perfunctory basic training. The Irish CMAC had a stark choice. It could become a professional service, responsible to the client and equal in standards to any other counselling service on offer, or it could languish into a second-class service which would let down the client and bring discredit to the church. His immediate task was to step up the entire training, basic and in-service. This called for much more than a one-man service unit. It would require a fully functional central office similar to that in London; something that, in his view, would not be possible without the approval and the support of the Episcopal Conference.

The Bishops' View

The bishops saw all this from a necessarily different perspective. They had two concerns. The first had to do with the status of the central office *vis-à-vis* the dioceses. While willing to grant the central office the absolute right to control standards, they were not prepared to vest in it any authority which could impinge on the ultimate authority of the bishop in his diocese. This attitude did not arise from pique or from political motives but, as we shall see in a following chapter, from the nature of a bishop's office in the church and the conventions which govern the procedure in the Episcopal Conference as a consequence.

The second was the question of the funding of the central office. The bishops had been led into a perception of a central office which, in dimension, had little relation to that envisaged by Fr Kennedy. They had readily accepted the concept of a one-man national office and director presented to them by Fr Browne and the INE in the memorandum of May 1975, and the obligation to fund it. The Director would be a priest to replace Fr O'Leary in the conduct of selections, overseeing the basic training and giving information talks. He would have an office and a clerk and get travelling expenses. The total cost quoted to government for grant purposes was £19,250. (In the memo to the Episcopal Conference the estimate quoted is £10,000. It is probable that the INE were then aware that a government cheque for £10,000 was in the post and quoted to the bishops in round figures the net cost to be met from episcopal funds). The bishops accepted in good faith what the INE in good faith told them. They could have no idea of the recent revolution in counselling which would call for a much more professional organisation and for the services of a super-enlarged central office. From the beginning Fr Kennedy's escalating demands put a strain on their limited resources. What they managed to do was most generous in the circumstances but they were never able to fund the office at the level it required.

The central office which emerged was a miracle of improvisation and adaptation and of judicious deployment of scarce resources. The achievement in those early years could only be described as extraordinary. This was due entirely to the commitment of the director and his priest assistants and to the generosity of a host of voluntary workers. Yet within this magnificent effort there lay a serious drawback. Its very success gave the illusion to many people, bishops amongst them, of being all that was required. The reality was that the office had all the character of stop-gap, day-to-day existence. It was housed in a redundant block of All Hallows College on a short term renewable lease. When the assistant priests left they were replaced by part-time lay staff. All senior lay posts were filled on short-term contracts, generally by pensioners or people near retirement. Forward planning and provision for future development were unknown luxuries.

The stop-gap syndrome became a chronic condition. There was no long-term provision for the solid, privately owned, permanent headquarters which would be a home and a centre to this nationwide professional organisation, nor for a future when the director and assistants at central office would be lay people with home and family demands, working normal office hours for an appropriate salary. It lacked two of the qualities held by the CMAC as necessary for the survival of a marriage – permanency and predictability! The underlying and ongoing problem was simply shortage of funds.[1]

An Indirect Authority

The preservation of the 'diocesan structure' by which each bishop founded and maintained the centres within his diocese conferred a degree of autonomy on the centres which in some respects rendered them independent of the central office. While the central office retained sole responsibility for the selection, enrolment, basic and inservice training of counsellors and, in theory, had adequate powers to enforce good standards in the delivery of the service, in practice it had only indirect influence in the management and practices of the centres. The central office could lay down guidelines, provide in-service training courses and organise annual conferences, but, in a voluntary service, it could only exhort centres to participate; it could not compel except as a last resort. Whilst the majority of centres and counsellors grasped at the opportunity to improve themselves, there was inevitably a minority who did not respond. Having to rely on powers of motivation and persuasion greatly increased the demands on the central office and in particular, on the National Director.[2]

CHAPTER 16

The Kennedy Years (1975-1984)

Fr Andy Kennedy, the first National Director in Ireland, was a man of extraordinary resources, physically, mentally and not least spiritually. In nine years under his direction CMAC Ireland was transformed from an assortment of disconnected centres with minimum training into a coherent professional organisation. It was a remarkable achievement in view of the fact that the central office was chronically short of funds. However his dream of founding a church-based service to Catholic marriage and family, from school to post-marriage, was never realised.

A Trainee National Director
As early as 1968 Fr O'Leary was keeping an eye out for a suitable priest to replace him on the Irish scene. His first target was Fr Robert Arthur, priest-chairman of the Waterford centre, whom he invited to go to London to learn the ropes. Fr Arthur declined because of his mother's illness. There is no record of further invitations until, sometime after 1969, Fr O'Leary spotted someone who was destined to play a major role in the development of CMAC in Ireland: Fr Andy Kennedy of the Cashel diocese. Fr Andy was released in 1971 by his bishop, Archbishop Thomas Morris,[1] to work in the CMAC headquarters in London where he remained until appointed National Director in Ireland in 1975. Born in Tipperary town, Fr Kennedy started his ministry as a curate in Dublin and later moved to Limerick city where he became for a time a lecturer in social studies and later a prison chaplain. At the time of his move to London he was director of the CMAC in his native diocese of Cashel and chairman of the INE.

Fr Kennedy was four years at London headquarters, the last two as head of training. At English conferences he became well known to the Irish contingent as the priest from their homeland; a fair-haired, stocky, quietly humorous man, of somewhat retir-

98

Canon O'Leary   *Fr Andy Kennedy*

ing disposition, thoughtfully observing proceedings from a seat in the background. Few were aware that he was there as an understudy to Fr O'Leary or thought of him then as the future National Director of the CMAC in Ireland.

Appointment as National Director of CMAC of Ireland
In May 1975 the first Irish assembly met and elected a National Executive Committee. The assembly also followed the INE's example by submitting Fr Kennedy's name to the Episcopal Conference for the post of National Director. On 25 June 1975 the Episcopal Conference, having approved a separate CMAC for Ireland, notified Fr Kennedy that he had been appointed National Director, though he did not take up the appointment until 6 November 1975. He was, however, preparing the ground and came over at least once to Dublin to meet the new NEC.

A Surprise for the New NEC
Shortly after their election the NEC had their first meeting. They elected Dr Jim Barnes (Dublin) chairman and Ann Small (Wexford) secretary. The other four were Fr Willie Lee (Cashel), Liam Murphy (Navan), John Kernan (Limerick), and Jim Hewison (Waterford). The committee also co-opted Dr Rory Dennis. It was a small but promising group of highly-regarded

professionals. Chairman Dr Jim Barnes, a GP who specialised in the psychosexual field, came from a distinguished Dublin medical family (his brother, Dr Joe Barnes, was mentioned by Canon O'Leary as one of the group of doctors who first invited him to Ireland) and had become immensely popular and respected in the organisation and an important link with the medical profession. Uniquely for a doctor at that time, Dr Barnes had undergone the selection process and completed the basic training course. As chairman Dr Barnes had plans to create a medical panel which would present a professional image of the CMAC to the public and encourage referrals from the doctors. He envisaged that doctors would be in a position to bring specific scientific literature to the attention of the counsellors and also provide advice on statistics and research.

After his appointment, Fr Kennedy came from London to meet the NEC and announced that, as the bishops' appointed National Director, he would be accountable directly to the Episcopal Conference. The NEC was less than happy with this unexpected development. As the elected executive they regarded themselves as the controlling body in the name of the assembly, in accordance with the terms of Fr Browne's memorandum of May 1975 to the bishops (which the bishops had accepted). Normally they would have expected the National Director to be directly accountable to them, the recognised line of management in all such organisations. Fr Kennedy saw it differently. In choosing to be responsible directly to the Episcopal Conference, he was following the traditional role of the priest to be accountable only to his bishop that would undeniably give him a position of control independent of the NEC. Marshall recounts how Fr Gorman similarly assumed control when he became the first priest chairman in England 'replicating the situation in a parish where the parish priest retains complete control'. (M 24) However, unlike the English CMAC (which from the beginning had a legal structure which secured the NEC's position as the ultimate authority), the Irish CMAC had no constitution to determine the line of command. In this situation, rather than have an unseemly confrontation, the NEC swallowed hard, adapted to its secondary role, and continued loyally to serve the organisation and their clients as before.

It would be wrong to attribute Fr Kennedy's decision merely to a desire to have total control. His reasons went much deeper. Fr Kennedy had a vision of the potential of the CMAC in Ireland which few others shared at that time and he needed the freedom to pursue it. He would have seen the Episcopal Conference as the key to the realisation of that vision and himself, as the priest responsible to them, the person best placed to win their support. It was undoubtedly an heroic decision because he alone knew the Herculean task ahead and, in the manner of the priest, was determined to devote all his energies to this God-given objective. There was no thought of monetary reward, of holidays and days of relaxation. From his memorandum to the secretary of the Episcopal Conference in September 1975, before taking up his office in Ireland, it is clear that he saw his role as priest director and that of the 'priest assistants' whom he hoped to recruit, to be totally available to the organisation. He asked for a headquarters to include residential accommodation for the director: 'In order that he may be available to the personnel when they need to contact him (particularly evenings and weekends) I recommend that the director (and any priest assistant who may join him in the future) live on the premises.' And so it came to pass. For the next nine years he lived over the shop giving every waking hour to work and prayer, building up the organisation.

Inevitably there was a negative side. His decision deprived the assembly and the NEC of the opportunity to mature in the role of policy makers within the discipline of responsible management. Normally the NEC's main preoccupation would be the acquisition of funds and how to operate within budgetary limits. As a result of Fr Kennedy's decision this vital function was left to himself to sort out with the bishops, placing an enormous additional burden on his shoulders. In practice the NEC would take responsibility for policy decisions and support its executive officer in carrying them out. In foregoing this process Fr Kennedy found no comparable support structure within the Episcopal Conference. His position became isolated. Writing to the bishops of the Pastoral Commission in November 1976 he refers to his seclusion, hoping for a more effective contact with the bishops: 'I would only like to add the personal feeling of the isolation from my principal advisors which an interim arrangement would remedy.'

None of these 'consequences' of Fr Kennedy's decision were to have any significant adverse effect on the organisation apart from imposing additional burdens on the clergy. It could indeed be argued that Fr Kennedy's was a good decision in that 'he travels faster who travels alone'. Not all NECs are supportive to an enterprising executive officer. However, Fr Kennedy's presupposition that the Episcopal Conference should underwrite the cost of the central office as an ongoing commitment did give rise to a serious problem. It was true that the Episcopal Conference, by accepting the terms of Fr Browne's memorandum of May 1975, implied agreement to 'continued financial support ... for the national office'. Their commitment, however, was on a scale that was minuscule in relation to what Fr Kennedy would ultimately require.

The struggle by the bishops and Fr Kennedy over the years to resolve the issue took the focus off the alternative and appropriate source of funding, which was the government in the South. Governments readily acknowledge the value of the marriage counselling service in the community and accept an obligation to make a contribution. (In London, and later in Northern Ireland, the central offices were established and are maintained on the basis of guaranteed government support.) It is arguable that had the NEC, under Dr Barnes, been responsible for the funding of the central office it would have more quickly, and as a lay organisation more effectively, turned to government (which had already agreed a token contribution) for adequate funding. This must be a matter of conjecture. In the event it would take many years of strenuous efforts by the bishops and of shoe-string management at central office before the Episcopal Conference got a substantial relief from government funds.

A Cumbersome System
The nine-year saga of Fr Kennedy and the Irish Episcopal Conference is too fraught to relate in detail at this time. The main problems were his frustration with what he termed the 'cumbersome structure' of the avenues of communication and his struggle to persuade the bishops of the need for a significant increase in funding and of the provision of suitable headquarters accommodation. These difficulties were a constant drain on

energies already taxed to the limit by the urgent work of raising standards in the organisation. Only someone with Fr Kennedy's undaunted tenacity and unfailing humour would have taken it on.

Central to his problems was that he had no access to the full Conference except through the bishops of the Pastoral Commission (which took the CMAC under its wing). His only recourse was to present his case to a formal meeting of the Pastoral Commission bishops which they would relay to the full Episcopal Conference. The first such meeting he had with the bishops of the Pastoral Commission was on 4 November 1976, exactly a year from taking up office. The second was ten months later on 1 September 1977. Fr Kennedy went alone to both meetings. At the first meeting the four bishops of the Commission were joined by three centre priests which, with Fr Kennedy, made a total of eight clergymen discussing the future of a predominantly lay organisation. The minutes or notes (taken by Fr Kennedy) indicate that the meetings were somewhat rambling and inconclusive, with no focus and no capacity for decision-taking. (A feature of these and other such clerical meetings is that they tended to be exploratory and any decisions or conclusions from either side would come later in a written follow-up.) Fr Kennedy had then to depend on the bishops of the Pastoral Commission to persuade the full Episcopal Conference, whose decisions would be communicated to him in due course by the Conference secretary. Small wonder that Fr Kennedy complained of the process as being 'cumbersome'!

Financial Reality

On 15 September 1975, before he took up office in Ireland, Fr Kennedy addressed a memorandum to Bishop McCormack (secretary to the Episcopal Conference) setting out the minimum requirements for the central office, in terms which made it clear that the INE concept which the bishops had approved was quite unrealistic in terms of the funding and accommodation required. It was not until the autumn meeting of the Episcopal Conference in 1978 that the case he presented came to the attention of the full Conference. The bishops were naturally concerned when they found that the estimated cost to them of the central office of £10,000 per annum, which they had accepted from the INE, had soared to £177,515 for 1981, according to the estimate prepared by Mr John McLaughlin their Financial Controller. Not surprisingly this enormous increase created tensions between the Conference and Fr Kennedy which were never quite resolved. On 30 March 1982, eight years after his appointment as director, Fr Kennedy was informed by Bishop McCormack that: 'it was decided that this year the Episcopal Conference would contribute £45,000 towards the expenses of CMAC at national level ... In the general discussion serious concern was expressed at the rapid increase in the budget for CMAC. It was decided that the overall funding of CMAC requires immediate attention ...'

Headquarters Accommodation

There was no less a gap between the bishops' perception of headquarters accommodation and the requirements set out by Fr Kennedy in his memorandum of September 1975. What the bishops offered, through Mr John McLaughlin, was an office in the complex for Episcopal Commissions in Dublin and living accommodation with the priests of the Communications Centre in nearby Pranstown House, then owned by the hierarchy. What Fr Kennedy had in mind, as we have seen, was a large private house with office accommodation for various headquarters staff, a 'possible six', and living accommodation for the director and his priest assistants. Although the bishops did eventually, if reluctantly, meet the escalating costs of the central office, they firmly drew the line at providing a private residence. A letter from Bishop Harty of the Pastoral Commission dated 2 December 1976, after Fr Kennedy's first meeting with them the previous month, removed the provision of a house from the agenda for the foreseeable future: 'I would say there is a consensus on the broad proposals for the working of the CMAC in Ireland but some hesitation on the question of residence, office accommodation, etc. The financial restraints of the present time affect our thinking generally. Besides the Irish church has put so much into bricks and mortar we are understandingly slow to invest in more buildings.'

Room at All Hallows

Characteristically, Fr Kennedy found the solution which met his immediate needs and which the bishops could accept. At first he worked without an office and depended for a time on friends for living accommodation. He then acquired temporary office and living accommodation in All Hallows College, engaged the faithful Patty Elkinson as his secretary and began, single-handedly, the mammoth tasks of putting the structure of the central office in place and getting the training programme under way. If he had faith that the Lord would provide then his faith was fully justified when, one day early in 1978, the Rector of All Hallows approached him and offered him an entire floor of O'Donnell House, a residential block in the complex, complete with furnished bedrooms, a kitchen and shower block. Fr Kennedy grasped the offer with both hands. He now had accommodation for staff and visitors as he originally planned, not only entirely suitable for all his needs but located in a most appropriate setting in the stately stone-built complex of a residential clerical college in spacious parkland on the north side of Dublin. All Hallows was to be the CMAC headquarters for many years. The Vincentian Fathers should be remembered for this very special contribution to Christian marriage and family in Ireland!

Achievements

Fr Kennedy's one-man crusade to persuade the Irish bishops to update their perception of the central office did not divert him from the main task of building the CMAC into a professional organisation by launching and advancing the training programmes. He revelled in the work and pursued it with great energy and unflagging good spirits. Affable and relaxed, he loved to see the people he had helped to select flower and grow from the training. This was his main motivation, coupled with an inner strength which came from prayer and faith and a conviction that the CMAC was a unique opportunity in the Catholic Church for a service to marriage and family. Its realisation became his mission to which he devoted every waking hour.

Because very little was done in the way of selection and training in 1975, there was a tremendous backlog when he took up duty in November of that year. His first Annual Report for 1976 shows that, in that first year, he had visited all the centres and their bishops, conducted 36 selection conferences of 637 candidates, set up 24 basic training courses, organised the training of 11 new tutors, and planned for more, organised three conferences (Annual, Doctors' and Nurses'), maintained active contact with outside organisations in England and in Ireland (nine in all including the various committees of the English CMAC) and laid plans for a similar programme for the following year, while responding to the myriad day-to-day demands of the office. It was a prodigious performance.

When he took up duty as director at the end of 1975 there were 35 centres opened or opening. When he left in 1984, there were 50, with 998 trained counsellors, of whom 66 were tutors, and 711 other professionals. Fr Kennedy laid plans to divide the service into five regions, each under a part-time officer in addition to the Northern Ireland 'region'. In 1983 the operating cost of the Dublin office was £130,715 and of the Belfast office £51,860. Remedial counselling, pre-marriage, schools, NFP and medical services, were active and expanding. From 1975 to the end of 1983 the number of people seen under all headings was almost half a million people.[2] Except for those close to him at central office, few people were aware of Fr Kennedy's achievements in these terms. The evidence is that unfortunately, due to lack of effective communication between the Episcopal Conference and the central office of the CMAC, the Irish bishops had no real idea of the extent of his achievements either.

In the style of Fr O'Leary in London, Fr Kennedy proceeded to build up a team at headquarters: typically he had 'anticipated' the bishops' approval by recruiting his first 'priest assistant', Fr Brendan McDonnell OSA, in July 1977. On 14 July 1977 Fr Kennedy notified the bishops of the Pastoral Commission that he had recruited Fr McDonnell, who was already selected and trained as a CMAC counsellor, and had sent him off to the Catholic University in Washington USA for a year's training in counselling (with the aid of the £16,000 grant from government). Fr McDonnell remained until May 1983, when he left to go on missionary work in Africa.

On 18 May 1979 Fr Kennedy sought and obtained the approval of the Episcopal Conference for the appointment of Fr

Colm O'Doherty, released for five years by Bishop Edward Daly of the Derry diocese. After completing a course of training in pastoral care and counselling at the Menninger Clinic in Kansas USA, Fr Colm took up duty as a member of the training team in December 1979. He succeeded Bert Mc Conville as head of training and returned to his diocese in 1986. These two priests were Fr Kennedy's fulltime 'priest assistants' at central office. Their appointment was in keeping with the terms of the policy document submitted by Fr Kennedy to the February 1978 Episcopal Conference (and in the traditional Catholic pattern of an organisation run by a priest!). 'It is intended to keep costs as low as possible by involving priests in the service at this time and also arranging, if possible, the secondment/early retirement from their employment of existing CMAC personnel of proven suitability. In this it is hoped to avoid both the costly expense of pension schemes as well as the less attractive features of professionalism.'

Among the voluntary workers were two Dublin men, Brian Howlett (one of the first tutors trained under Doctors Marshall and Dominian in England) and Darach Connolly, who were in the team that conducted the first Irish tutor training course. Darach, a lawyer, later took a leading part in drafting the constitution. These two, with Bert McConville, a former lecturer in a Scottish Teacher Training College and head of training, Brian's wife Mary Howlett, Anne Nolan of Carlow and Fr Colm O'Doherty made up the first training team. Dr Esther Bradley became head of medical services, assisted by two salaried NFP specialists on her staff, Mary Higgins and Dorothy Scally. Sheila Campbell, founder of schools courses in relationships education in Belfast, became head of the service to schools. Fr McDonnell, Sean Holohan and I structured a new basic training course which for the first time included residential courses and experiential training. Of these helpers the gifted Brian Howlett became a stalwart of the headquarters team. He initiated the training programme and drew up the scheme for the first residential in-service training courses in 1976. Dr Jim Barnes was the first Irish CMAC specialist in psychosexual counselling. Peter Nugent, a future head of training, was Irish correspondent and later editor of the *Bulletin* in London. The first regional officers (appointed

after Fr Kennedy's retirement), were Anne Nolan, Carlow;
Gerry Cronin, Nenagh; Ita McCraith, Dublin; Clare D'Arcy Sligo
and Joe Dineen, Kerry.

One of Fr Kennedy's first tasks was to augment the tutor
body. There were six selected for tutor training in the final year
of the INE. They were Beverly Carbery, Carlow; Celine Regan,
Dublin; Elizabeth Roddy, Galway; Sean Holohan, Cashel; Paddy
McCarthy, Limerick and Peter Nugent, Dublin. To these he
added Dr Esther Bradley, Derry; Pat King, Derry; Frankie
Macnally, Belfast; Ita O'Sullivan, Cork and Margaret Watchhorn,
Dublin, making eleven in all, the first Irish tutors to be trained in
Ireland rather than England. The training was conducted by
Rina and Tony Howard from London, assisted by Brian Howlett
and Darach Connolly, over a series of weekends at Bellinter.
These eleven in addition to ten existing tutors trained in
England (see Appendix 2) were the first of the Irish tutor body
which he increased to nearly seventy before he retired in 1984,
an extraordinary talented and committed group which became
his power base for the raising of standards throughout the organisation.

Milestones
The Constitution: Not least of Fr Kennedy's achievements was
the negotiation of a constitution to the satisfaction of the
Episcopal Conference in 1981. The idea of a constitution was
never very high on Fr Kennedy's list of priorities, but the bishops had been pressing for one. Bishop McCormack wrote to Fr
Kennedy on 15 April 1978 on behalf of the Episcopal
Conference. While assuring Fr Kennedy of 'the support and confidence of the bishops and their appreciation (of the CMAC) and
the vital contribution it makes to the pastoral work of the church
in Ireland', he stated that the immediate requirement is a draft
constitution, adding, in this context, 'that in any future reorganisation of CMAC the diocesan structure and format, as it is in
Ireland, [must] be preserved'. It took years of tortuous negotiation before a draft acceptable to the bishops was agreed; it came
into effect, for a trial period of three years, on 1 February 1981.[3] A
feature of the constitution, apart from consolidating the authority
of the bishops, was the provision for an autonomous adminis-

tration in the North while preserving the unity of the organisation as an all-Ireland entity.

Northern Ireland Office: In 1982 Fr Kennedy established a separate administration in Belfast for the Northern Ireland centres
with the help of substantial grants from the government there
towards the foundation costs, including premises and running
costs. I was the first administration officer, succeeded in 1985 by
Jim Meehan, in 1988 by Mary McFadden, and in 1998 by Deirdre
O'Rawe.

Oireachtas, 1984: In 1983 the government in the South set up
an all-party committee on marriage and family and the problems arising from marriage breakdown. The CMAC had no op-
tion but to make a submission. Inevitably there were expectations that, as a church sponsored organisation, it would reiterate
the Catholic Church stand on marriage and divorce. In the event
the submission, crafted largely by Fr Kennedy in consultation
with the church's marriage tribunals (at the request of the
Episcopal Conference), was a brief document which refrained
from political pronouncements and confined itself to the reali-
ties of marriage for those involved. At the committee's invitation, a follow-up verbal submission was made on 6 June 1984 by
a team led by Darach Connolly in which the need for relationships education in secondary schools was emphasised. The pre-
sentations were acclaimed by the committee as the most cogent
and persuasive they had received, a fact which was amply
demonstrated in the final report. The outcome owed much to Fr
Kennedy's shrewd judgement and his undoubted abilities in the
field of public relations.

The Tutor-Per-Centre Scheme: As we have seen, the central office did not directly intervene in the management of centres
which were under the control of the local bishops. Whilst the
central office was responsible for the selection and enrolment of
counsellors and their basic training, once the counsellors began
work at the centres their attendance at further training courses
or conferences was at the discretion of the centres. This created a
division between the authority of the central office in the en-
forcement of standards and the autonomy of the centres in running the service. To bridge this gap Fr Kennedy inaugurated a
scheme which became known by the unwieldy title of the 'tutor-

per-centre' scheme by which a tutor was designated to each centre. It proved to be an inspired move. While the tutors' main
purpose was to conduct training exercises at the centres and encourage participation at further training courses, they discovered themselves in the additional and no less important role as a
personal support to the centre and evidence of recognition of the
centres by the central office. Nothing did so much to unify the
organisation and to elevate the standards of counselling as the
tutor-per-centre scheme.

A Dream that was Dreamed in the Heart
From his first days as director, Fr Kennedy had a vision of the
central office becoming the foundation of a form of church-
sponsored 'marital institute' which would conduct research into
all aspects of marriage and family in Ireland, and which would
advise government and implement remedial and support measures. He felt it could be the springboard for a church support
system for Christian family from school through to post-marriage. Funding should be available from the state, already financing such institutions as the Health Education Bureau and
the Irish Management Institute, but directly committed under
its constitution to the support of marriage and family.
Encouraged by government soundings on the possibility of the
CMAC supplying an NFP service financed by the Department of
Health, Fr Kennedy produced an outline for consideration by
the bishops in June 1978. The tenor of his suggestion was that
the state should be asked to fund the central office *in toto* in
recognition of the church's initiative in providing at immense
cost this vital service to marriage and family in Ireland.[4] His tim-
ing was unfortunate. The bishops of the Pastoral Commission,
already involved in the uphill task of persuading the Episcopal
Conference to adjust to a much more magnified version of a
CMAC central office, were in no mood to entertain or advocate
any more soaring visions from Fr Kennedy. The dream ended
there.

The Final Submission
On his departure in September 1984, Fr Kennedy circulated a
letter to each of the Irish bishops giving his views on their contri-

bution to the CMAC during his term of office. For the individual bishops he had nothing but praise. It was due to the initiative of each bishop and the support of their priests that the CMAC was now, for the most part, established and thriving in every diocese in the country. 'In a word, the moral authority of the bishop of each diocese has been indispensable to the growth of the CMAC and for that the bishops (active, retired and deceased) deserve to be commended.' He was, however, disappointed by what he saw as lack of support by the bishops in the Episcopal Conference, deploring the 'absence of a collective mind or will on the part of the Episcopal Conference'.

His Legacy

Fr Kennedy was gifted with many innate qualities of leadership. He had a genius for spotting and recruiting talent, and once the person was appointed, of non-interference. He had humour and was fun to be with, and his uncanny ability to remember names, including the names of spouses and children, fostered a family spirit which bonded the whole organisation. His care for each was manifest and genuine. During his directorship there were no schisms, no walk-outs. His abiding concern throughout was for the standard of service in the CMAC which, for him, could never be high enough. When he left he had accomplished what he set out to do: to establish the principle of excellence and to put in place a system to guarantee that it would be achieved and would endure.

Postscript

Fr Kennedy retired in 1984 to take up a one-year course in Spiritual Direction at Loyola University in Chicago. He returned to his native diocese and was appointed curate in Cappaghmore, Co Limerick. He left there in 1989 to serve the Church in Alabama, USA. He is, at time of writing, a PP in Our Lady of Lourdes Church, Birmingham, Alabama.

CHAPTER 17

The bishops and the CMAC

When the bishops of Ireland meet in the Episcopal Conference, they meet as independent principals, who confer on matters of common interest but always on the principle that nothing that transpires in the Conference will supersede the ultimate authority of each individual bishop within his diocese. This fact had important implications for the authority of the central office of the CMAC.

An Exceptional Achievement

At the 27th annual conference of Accord in Limerick, 1996, 34 years after the first centre opened in Ireland, Bernard McDonagh (Secretary of the Department of Equality and Law Reform in the Republic) addressed the conference with these words: 'Because of the size and extent of Accord's network of counselling centres, it is the principal agency for marriage and family counselling in this country. There is no part of Ireland where you do not operate. Yours is a unique organisation in that it provides a voluntary counselling service of the highest professional standard. Accord is particularly noted for the rigour of its selection process for counsellors. The success of Accord is an extremely good example of the positive and practical way in which the Catholic Church tackles the issue of marriage breakdown ... Of course, Accord does not just provide marriage counselling services. You can counsel people in fertility and family planning as well as providing excellent marriage preparation courses.'

Mr McDonagh was referring to the 1200 trained voluntary (CMAC) counsellors in 58 centres throughout Ireland, North and South, under the new name of Accord. The Irish bishops could look with satisfaction at this pastoral service which they and they alone had established, centre by centre in their dioceses, in response to the needs of their flock. The bishops who established the first CMAC centres could hardly have foreseen that this unique lay organisation in the church would eventually grow to national dimensions and make such an enormous professional contribution in the area of marriage and family.

The Benign Authority

The involvement of the CMAC, a predominantly lay organisation, in the sensitive pastoral area of marriage and family was a progressive movement on the bishops' part, in keeping with the changes in the church in the aftermath of Vatican II. There was an added sensitivity in those years following *Humanae Vitae* (1968), due to the presence in the Catholic community of a number who openly challenged the church's teaching on birth control. Even so there are very few instances of a bishop intervening in the affairs of a centre or of the central office. The few that did occur had no connection with the promotion of false doctrine. Otherwise the bishops were notable for their non-interference – except to write the cheques! In fact it was this benign attitude of the bishops at centre level, and their generous financial support, that made it possible for the central office to pursue more advanced basic and in-service training programmes after 1975.

The Priest-Chairman

In practice each bishop appointed a trusted priest to represent him at the centre and, as is the way with the clergy, gave him a free hand. And so was born the office, peculiar to the CMAC in the early years, of the 'priest-chairman'. Priest-chairmen came in all shapes and sizes and had a major influence on the welfare of the centre. Most were sensible, concerned men who worked hard to make the centre a success; some indeed were blessed with a special gift for the job and went on later to higher things. A few, inevitably, were less well suited and did nothing to facilitate the growth of the centre. Marshall recalls similar problems with English centres and how 'not infrequently the difficulties related to the priest chairman of the centre and needed intervention by the director'. (M 36) In the course of time, it became the practice, in England and in Ireland, for centres to elect a lay chairperson with the 'centre priest' attending as the bishop's representative.

The Episcopal Conference

The support of the individual bishops for their CMAC centres was less evident in the relationship between the Episcopal Conference and the central office of the CMAC. In 1975, when the Conference approved the establishment of a separate Irish CMAC with its own director and central office, there developed an unprecedented, and almost certainly unforeseen situation by which the Episcopal Conference became involved in the policies and management of the central office, a function for which the Conference was manifestly unsuited.

One of the many misconceptions about the Catholic Church is that there is a chain of command from the Pope through the cardinals and the canons down to the lowly curate. In fact there is effectively but one link in the chain; the Pope appoints the bishop who is directly responsible to him. The bishop has total autonomy within his diocese. Other church titles may confer status and certain privileges on the holder but never a right of intervention into the domain of a bishop. The effect of this ancient tradition in the church is far-reaching.

Each bishop runs his diocese as an independent state and is accorded absolute sovereignty by fellow bishops, a principle which the bishops extend to each other in the Episcopal Conference. The Episcopal Conference is therefore an occasion where bishops meet as independent equals, whose first 'rule' is that no bishop is bound by any decision of the others. Any perception of the Episcopal Conference as bishops acting in concert is misleading. They can and do reach broad agreement on church matters and make pronouncements in the name of the Conference. However, any collective assent to the foundation of a body operating with the authority of the Conference, such as the central office of the CMAC, would be on the implicit understanding that such a body must defer at all times to the authority of the local bishop in his diocese. It follows that the central office, as a creature of the Episcopal Conference, is precluded from exercising overall control of the organisation throughout the country, a restriction which would not apply if it had independent status.

In the 1970s the Irish Episcopal Conference met twice yearly. Proceedings were conducted in private and they did not normally receive deputations. (A notable exception was when they had Eithne McGuire of the CMAC give an information talk, which had a very positive reception, to the Episcopal Conference in Mulrany in 1974.) The Conference conducts its business with the outer world mainly through sub-committees or commissions (such as the Pastoral Commission which then took the CMAC central office under its umbrella). Commissions report to the Conference for further consideration or for affirmation where appropriate. The commissions are financed through the Finance and General Purposes Committee of the hierarchy from funds provided by the dioceses and which are administered by a Financial Controller.

The Episcopal Conference is, therefore, a consultative body, with no pretensions or capacity to operate as an administrative unit similar to a board of directors. There were real problems when Fr Kennedy began reporting to it as if it had an administrative function. An example was the withholding of approval of a staff appointment made by the director and the NEC and approved by the two bishops of the Pastoral Commission, 'pending further clarification', regardless of the fact that it would be six months before the next full meeting!

The Pre-marriage Courses
The absence of effective contact with the Episcopal Conference led to the occasional breakdown in communications. An example was the introduction of the marriage regulations in 1983, without any consultation with the CMAC, which required the couple, amongst other things, to attend a pre-marriage course. According to Pastoral Guidelines: 'In Ireland (this) means a pre-marriage course under the aegis of the CMAC (set up by the bishops for the purpose) or a similar course of instruction.' The centres were quite unprepared for the inevitable problems which this caused.

The pre-marriage courses were usually constructed in a series of integrated sessions, about five or so, the first being devoted to breaking the ice, dispelling preconceived fears about the course and inducing a relaxed atmosphere. Vital to the process was the willing participation of the couples – not difficult to achieve when couples had come voluntarily. It was a totally different situation when the group included couples resentful at being required to be there and some determined not to co-operate. Another problem was couples arriving without notice on the instructions of their priest (who might have no knowledge of the format of the course) expecting to be admitted at the midway stage.

Similar regulations were introduced by bishops in Britain without consulting the CMAC there, apparently oblivious of the problems that 'compulsory attendance' would create at the pre-marriage courses. Marshall records that: 'When some dioceses made a rule that couples intending to marry must give six months notice to their parish priest and must attend a CMAC course, CMAC was overwhelmed. The latter requirement was introduced without any prior consultation with CMAC. The result in some centres was chaos; a centre which had for years run a course with an average attendance of four couples was suddenly faced with 72 people for whom they did not have physical accommodation, let alone counsellors to handle so large a number. Moreover, some of the couples resented having to attend, which was not a good starting point for a counselling approach; the entire time could be taken up by exploring why they resented being there.' (M 92)

Problems of Finance
Among the bishops there was concern about getting involved in projects where costs could escalate. A previous effort to establish a central fund to finance the various episcopal commissions had painful memories and a history which amply demonstrated the robust independence of the individual bishops. Fr Joe Dunn describes the bishops' problems of raising funds in 1967 to finance the Communications Centre. The hierarchy had set their face against a national collection and offered instead to levy each diocese for 'a contribution to a common fund which would support the various national commissions ... Unfortunately John Charles McQuaid, Archbishop of Dublin, would not agree to pay his full share, and the other bishops were not willing to accept that he shouldn't. So nobody paid – key members of the hierarchy wanted certain activities to be continued but the hierarchy as a whole couldn't agree to pay for them.'[1]

While a fund was in place by 1975, it was not unlimited and there was always the possibility that some bishops would react adversely to escalating demands. In this regard Fr Kennedy's estimates for the central office of the CMAC were a source of great unease to the Episcopal Conference and remained so throughout his nine years as director. On 29 November 1980 Bishop McCormack informed Fr Kennedy that, at a recent meeting of the Conference, many bishops commented: 'that the figures in the budgets submitted seemed somewhat inflated and were not in line with the figures found in the budgets prepared by other Commissions and agencies.'

The bishops had before them a budget prepared by Fr Kennedy for the Department of Health and were obviously disturbed by the sums involved. At that stage the central office had run up a deficit of £30,000. In the absence of any other source of funds the assembly had decided this deficit could only be cleared by a levy of £700 on each centre. The bishops approved, but only for this occasion. They asked their Financial Controller, Mr John McLaughlin, to make an examination of the financing of the CMAC and prepare a budget for 1981, making it clear that while they would be prepared to increase their contribution to the central office, they would not decide on a figure 'until decisions have been taken on the development proposals and a firm indication received from the Department of Health on the level of financial support they propose to give to the work of the CMAC ... The Episcopal Conference is very conscious of the importance of CMAC in the area of family apostolate but it is not willing to give an open-ended commitment to financing future developments until a clearer picture emerges.'

Mr McLaughlin's budget for 1981 for running expenses and proposed developments totalled £177,515 (less grants). What this did for the Episcopal peace of mind is not recorded but subsequent records show that the body of bishops in the Episcopal Conference never became reconciled to this degree of funding of the CMAC central office.

An Unsuitable Assignment

There is no evidence that the Episcopal Conference ever intended to establish any degree of control of the CMAC central office.

The indications are that their involvement, in this capacity, arose as a consequence of Fr Kennedy's decision as director to be accountable directly to the Conference and not to the NEC. Apparently neither he nor the bishops (nor indeed the NEC or the assembly) realised the full implications of his decision: that he was involving the Episcopal Conference in an area of management which that body was not designed to handle and a degree of expenditure which it did not anticipate.

The decisive moment was the acceptance by Bishop McCormack, secretary to the Episcopal Conference, of a memorandum from Fr Kennedy in September 1975 setting out his requirements for the central office. By accepting the memorandum for consideration by the Episcopal Conference Bishop McCormack, by implication, involved the Conference in responsibility for the management (and the financing) of the CMAC central office, and, more importantly, accepted Fr Kennedy's chosen position as being directly responsible to the Episcopal Conference and not to his Executive Committee. An alternative would have been to return the memorandum to Fr Kennedy to refer to his Executive Committee and let the committee take it up with the bishops if it so decided.

History Made

Nevertheless, it was the bishops who first recognised the need for a specialised service to marriage and family and took steps to provide it. In doing so they involved lay people in unprecedented numbers into the pastoral service of the church and opened a whole new area of co-operation between clergy and laity in the area of family apostolate. In establishing and maintaining the CMAC the bishops have written a new chapter in the history of the church in Ireland.

CHAPTER 18

Reflections on the CMAC (Ireland)

By Nicholas Tyndall

Nicholas Tyndall became a marriage counsellor in 1962 and was Chief Officer of the National Marriage Guidance Council from 1968 to 1986. His wife, Elizabeth, and two sons are priests of the Anglican Church in England. During his years with NMGC Nicholas Tyndall maintained a close and friendly relationship with the CMAC in England and in Ireland. He shares here some reflections on his experience of our organisation.

One of my great pleasures on becoming Chief Officer of NMGC in 1968 was to visit the CMAC office in Landsdowne Rd, London, to meet my opposite number in CMAC, the benign and skull-capped Fr Maurice O'Leary. We went on to meet regularly and share ideas informally, often as a threesome with Douglas Woodhouse, Director of what is now known as the Tavistock Institute of Marital Studies. David Mace, my predecessor, claimed that NMGC had played a positive role in getting CMAC established as a separate body in 1946, but the two bodies had drifted far apart.

The renewal of a creative partnership led to my attendance at CMAC conferences in England. When *Humanae Vitae* first appeared, I remember Jack Dominion asserting that it left the vexed question of contraception to individual consciences – not without some dissension! I have fond memories of the evenings, indeed nights, being taken over by the Irish contingent with their harps and songs and humorosity. And I well remember everything stopping for the Mass, with the long procession of white-robed priests signifying the essential difference between NMGC and CMAC. Alas, for me, the day when CMAC (Ireland) started holding its own conferences, for, without the Irish, the English events could never match the spontaneous *ceilidhs*. Thereafter delegates went to bed on serious discussion.

CMAC (Ireland) is associated in my mind with large echoing seminaries. Fr Andy Kennedy was so proud when he established the first CMAC office in a corner of one in Dublin and the conferences took place in rural seminaries. I recollect when one of the chief legal officers of state came to address the conference, and a priest in the audience mentioned the problems he faced arising from the gap between church and state regulations on marriage. Was he an accessory to bigamy if he celebrated a church wedding of a partner who had a previous state marriage which was not recognised by the church? 'You're a man of the cloth,' replied the Minister, 'so do what's right by the church. I'm a man of the law, so you leave the law to me. Next question?' Such unresolved personal dilemmas seemed very much part of these gatherings! I always came away feeling that CMAC filled a vital role as a sentient group for liberal-minded couples and priests, where they could be open about difficulties in their own relationships and the struggle to reconcile their own values within the constraints of the doctrine of the Catholic Church.

CMAC's role as a lively, fermenting group within the church meant that it didn't matter that there seemed to be few clients! CMAC workers were keen to be counsellors, regardless of consumer demand – or lack of it! Much time and care was given to training, but I feared that if a couple with a problem did turn up in a centre they were in danger of being swooped on with undue enthusiasm. Seriously, though, I thought that all the marriage guidance agencies were over-anxious about being professional and fell into the danger of following models of work which were inappropriate. In NMGC we became elitist through too great a copying of the psychodynamic approach of the Tavistock. We expected our clients to have proper 'counselling' problems. And marriage education always seemed to be a poor second to counselling. In its turn, CMAC in England modelled itself on NMGC. It gave undue precedence to office-based confidential counselling rather than pioneering the development of more informal pastoral care within their churches. And I felt that CMAC in Ireland was too slavishly following the English model and not managing to capitalise on the strength that came from being an adjunct of the national church. This is probably no longer so. Certainly in my time marriage preparation was a foremost activity in CMAC and I was impressed and envious when it was reported that over half the couples marrying in Dublin had been on a CMAC pre-marriage course. And I believe (for my last contact with CMAC was 10 years ago) that CMAC also now maximises the potential that exists within the church structure for offering non-problem type help to married couples and individuals.

And, lo and behold, why the craze, started by *Relate* (ugh!) to change names and get out from under 'Marriage'? The unique expertise of the organisations is in issues relating to marriage. I suspect the name changes reflect a wobbling of professional confidence. (Interestingly the M.G. Centre in London went independent and still calls itself London Marriage Guidance.)

But enough of the questions. My abiding memory of CMAC in Ireland is of the warmth and delight of the people involved, the enormous sense of love and concern for humanity, the commitment, enthusiasm and strength to persevere in spite of setbacks. A strength typified for me by one memory of going with a CMAC couple to an International Conference on the birth of a baby, entitled 'When 2 becomes 3'. When asked why they were being a bit quiet, the wife replied, 'Well, we were looking forward to the conference, but we've just learnt that 6 is to become 7!'

Thanks for your friendship over many years, and congratulations to all involved in the development of CMAC/ACCORD in Ireland.

Nicholas Tyndall, July 1996.

CHAPTER 19

Marriage Counselling in the CMAC

A Change in the Perception of Counselling

In 1946 the Catholic Marriage Advisory Council, as the name implies, began as an organisation to advise people with marriage problems in the accepted mode of the time when priests, doctors, lawyers, head teachers and similar authority figures were seen as the proper people to approach when help was needed. The first helpers in the CMAC were known as 'consultants' who gave their clients advice and assistance in the conventional social-work model, or, if necessary, referred them to a more qualified expert. The advent of Carl Rogers' theory of client-centred counselling (popularly known as non-directive counselling) changed all that. Marshall records that the shift from the social work approach to Rogerian counselling came about through the friendship and continuing contact in the first years between Graham-Green, Chairman of CMAC, and Dr David Mace, Director of NMGC (a contact discouraged by the priest representing Cardinal Griffin on the executive). 'These influences, coupled with the vision of Graham-Green, enabled CMAC to avoid being trapped in a Catholic ghetto.' (M 78)

Counselling is one of those words which has subtly changed its meaning in recent years. The dictionary defines counselling as 'advising or giving advice'. In common parlance, however, the word has become a specialised term in the field of psychotherapy, referring in particular to 'Rogerian' or 'client-centred' non-directive counselling, in which 'counselling' and 'giving advice' are mutually exclusive.

From Freud to Rogers

Counselling as a therapy was pioneered by the father of psychoanalysis and psychotherapy, Sigmund Freud (1856-1939). Freud called the process 'transference', or the displacement of feelings, a process in which he listened to the patient with complete detachment, refusing to play along or respond to the patient's expectations, thus inducing in the patient a 'second neurosis' which he would then interpret. His objective was to bring into the conscious mind patterns in the unconscious affecting the patient's behaviour. Freud's inspired philosophy of human nature provided the basis for the first therapeutic procedures for modifying behaviour. While his therapeutic approaches have inevitably been extended or modified over the years, his theories remain as a benchmark against which all subsequent developments in the field of psychoanalysis are measured.

A dramatic modification of Freud's approach to psychotherapy was introduced in the early 1940s by the American psychologist Carl R Rogers (1902-1987). Rogers' theory was based on his belief in the innate capacity of the patient to resolve his or her own problems. It was the function of the therapist to enable the patient to achieve this goal. Contrary to Freud's 'detachment' from the patient, the key to the Rogerian process was the therapist's relationship with the patient, and the avoidance of any intervention or guidance which would undermine the patient's capacity or right to self-direction. While the process did not preclude the giving of information as appropriate, it was subject always to the inviolable principle of the client's right of self-determination, a concept which was to have a revolutionary impact in the field of psychotherapy.

Rogers was always his own man. From his student days he had an instinct to question accepted dogmas and the courage to change and act on his own judgement. In his college years his interests changed from agriculture to history, to religion and, finally, to clinical psychology. During his religious studies he realised that he could not go along with the religious thinking of his parents, a seminal decision from which, he believed, he derived his psychological independence. As a clinical psychologist he specialised in child guidance and held several academic appointments from 1939 to 1964, when he joined the staff of the Western Behavioural Sciences Institute in La Jolla, California, to work in the field of human relations.

Here he developed the person-centred approach to many areas of human relationships, including the resolution of conflicts in society, which earned him a nomination for the Nobel prize shortly before he died. It was in the field of psychotherapy, however, that he gained worldwide recognition. Rogers startled his contemporaries when he challenged the accepted Freudian approach of the therapist as the 'physician' making a diagnosis and prescribing for the 'patient'. He saw the 'patient' rather as a 'client' who comes voluntarily to the 'counsellor' for help with a problem without surrendering his or her responsibility for the situation or his right to make his own decisions. Rogers' basic assumption was that within every person there is a trustworthy positive centre, resourceful and capable of self-direction.[1] The counsellor must see the client as a person having worth and dignity and the right to make his or her own decisions and not 'an object to be dissected, diagnosed and manipulated'.[2]

The Spiritual Dimension of Rogers and Some Misunderstandings
Whilst Rogers' concepts were derived from humanistic psychology they had a remarkable spiritual import for Christians 'with eyes to see', a fact which had particular implications for the CMAC. After eighteen years as Director of the CMAC, Canon O'Leary recalled the impact of his first acquaintance with Rogers when he took up the work in 1956. He began to see Rogerian counselling as 'very much in line with all in which I had been trained, and yet never realised what it was I had been trained in ...'[3] Forty years later, Fr Gerard W Hughes SJ echoes his sentiments: 'Carl Rogers advocated an attitude of "unconditional positive regard" in the listener, no matter who the client might be ... But then I began to see God in this way, a God who is always for us, and this had an immediate effect on my prayer. God is no longer remote, no longer primarily interested in my failings ... Words can make the soul sing. Carl Rogers, the unbeliever, did this for me.'[4]

In his history of the CMAC in England, Professor Marshall records the significance of the adoption of the Rogerian approach in the late 1940s: 'Rogerian counselling was a radical change. Instead of people being told or advised what to do, they were helped both to discover themselves, and to discover for themselves, what they should do. Many Catholics, including priests, found this approach difficult to understand. They believed the CMAC should be spelling out the "teachings of the church"; they did not appreciate that people with problems often knew, only too well, the teaching of the church, but did not see how they could follow it. The process of counselling was to help them in this situation. This basic misunderstanding was a source of constant friction between CMAC and some elements in the church.' (M 78-79)

These frictions did not arise to the same extent in Ireland because by the time the first centre opened in Belfast in 1962, non-directive counselling was firmly established as the basis of remedial counselling everywhere, including the CMAC. Occasionally a clerical objection was raised, but rarely from within the CMAC ranks. Belfast was something of an exception in that it was established as a diocesan agency, the Down and Connor Marriage Advisory Service, separate from the main body of the CMAC. While the selection and training was conducted by Fr O'Leary and his CMAC team from London, it was evident from the beginning that the centre intended to present the image of a Catholic organisation upholding Catholic doctrine. In his initial address to the new counsellors Bishop Philbin reminded them of their 'special duty to society as Catholics ... to uphold the principles of natural law'.[5]

A Role for the Laity

An important effect of the Rogerian principles of counselling was to open the door for 'ordinary people' to act as marriage counsellors. Most married people reacted with incredulity to their invitation to become helpers to people with marriage problems. They had enough problems keeping their own marriages together! An introduction to Rogers, however, showed them that one does not have to be a Solomon to relieve suffering. What was needed was the right personal disposition, together with training in the practice and principles of non-directive counselling.

Biestek

These principles were set out in a small handbook, *The Casework*

Relationship, by Frederick P Biestek, a Jesuit attached to The School of Social Work in Loyola University, Chicago. From the late 1950s it became a textbook for CMAC basic training. With some misgivings, Biestek set about applying a set of rules to the 'living pulsating thing' that is the casework relationship: '... the skill to establish and maintain a good casework relationship is eminently more important than the ability to define it.'[6] Biestek considered that it would nevertheless help students to have a concept of the main elements of a good casework relationship. In this compact and readable handbook he set out, defined and analysed these seven basic needs of the person seeking help: to be treated as an individual; to be allowed full expression of feelings; to be given a sympathetic response; to be recognised as a person of worth; not to be judged; to be free to make choices and decisions; and, finally, to be treated in strict confidence. In short, the client should feel valued, accepted and safe.

A misinterpretation

The popular label 'non-directive counselling', gave rise to some misunderstanding, within and without the CMAC, in that it implied an aimless drift, with the counsellor adopting a sphinx-like attitude of non-interference. (The term, 'client-centred counselling', was much less misleading in this respect.) This misconception, Rogers asserts, 'usually held by counsellors with little specific training ... has led to considerable failure in counselling ... and for good reasons. In the first place, the passivity and seeming lack of interest or involvement is experienced by the client as rejection, since indifference is in no real way the same as acceptance. In the second place, a *laissez-faire* attitude does not in any way indicate to the client that he is regarded as a person of worth.'[7] The counsellor's attitude and response to the client plays a crucial part in the process. The counsellor must listen with continuous attention, striving to get inside the client's feelings, and resisting all temptation to make diagnoses and guide the client. Such professional instincts are subjugated to the central purpose: to convey to the client, in sensitive and measured tones, a feeling of being genuinely understood and accepted.

The Importance of Selection

The attitudes and codes of such a counsellor are formed by an inherent deep respect for, and acceptance of, the individual and the right of the individual to make choices, a philosophy of life which, in Rogers' words, 'is most likely to be held by the person who has a basic respect for the worth and significance of himself'.[8] The counsellor's 'operational techniques' will reflect these inner values and will develop through life in relation to the counsellor's own struggle for personal growth and integration. The necessity of ensuring that prospective counsellors have these essential attributes has given rise to the complex and exhaustive selection procedures which are now a feature of recruitment to the CMAC and to other counselling agencies.

Egan: the Dawn of a New Era

In the 1960s the CMAC counsellors 'qualified' by their selection and by undergoing a good grounding in the principles of Rogerian counselling. Nevertheless, there persisted amongst the CMAC tutor body and headquarters staff a nagging concern about the application of counselling in practice. The problem was that there was no way of monitoring what went on in the counselling room. Counsellors were bound to silence and clients invariably do not talk. Rogers was strong on principles but short on specifics. He did however provide examples to illustrate appropriate as opposed to inappropriate responses, and recommended making and reviewing notes, or indeed recordings of interviews, in the context of ensuring that the counsellor was not unconsciously guiding the client.[9]

In the mid 1970s there appeared a new prophet in the counselling domain who was to become the CMAC's guiding light of counselling practice. He was Fr Gerard Egan, a gifted teacher and prolific writer of textbooks in counselling skills, and later Professor of Psychology and Organisational Studies at Loyola University in Chicago. Egan's theories and methodology owed much to Robert Carkhuff,[10] who had been a pupil of Carl Rogers, and whose systematic model of counselling stayed entirely true to the Rogerian principles of the client's self-direction.

Egan adopted and developed the Carkhuff system, preserving the Rogerian principles with the qualification that the client's fundamental need was a change of direction – to find a way out of a crisis or at least a more fulfilling way of life. Because counselling was non-directive it did not have to lack direction. It served no purpose for the counsellor to collude with the client round in a cycle of inadequacy – 'mulberry-bushing' as Egan called it! In his view, ineptness of this order on the counsellor's part not merely rendered the process futile but could actually make matters worse by compounding the client's sense of inability to cope. The counsellor had a responsibility to be effective in terms of enabling the client to recognise new opportunities and ways to alternative life styles.

Egan's theory was based on the belief that the profession of counselling called for skills of a high order, skills which should be acquired in training, especially experiential training, and supervised practice. These skills were based essentially on transactional analysis – the counsellor's ability to recognise the import of every communication with the client. Nothing was left to chance. The posture adopted by the counsellor, the eye contact, even the body language, all had a significance. Every response by the counsellor, verbal or otherwise, contributed to an interaction which had the potential to open the client to new ways of seeing things and discovering unused resources and new opportunities. Egan listed and classified a whole catalogue of interactions and responses from which the student could draw.

Egan saw three basic skills essential for effective counselling: *perceptiveness:* the ability to form an accurate perception of the client's worldview including contradictions and blind spots; *know-how:* the verbal facility to present these insights with sensitivity and regard for the client's feelings, and finally, the quality most difficult in practice: *assertiveness:* the acumen to recognise an opportunity to open another door in the client's view of the world and the authority to challenge the client at the appropriate moment even at the risk of making the client uncomfortable. Whilst the client's sense of warmth, respect and acceptance in the helper is a vital component of counselling, such good feelings in themselves are no evidence of real progress. 'It is much better if clients feel good because of what they accomplish in their day-to-day lives rather than because of what happens in the helping sessions themselves. Indeed ... helping sessions may at times be painful. In counselling, pain is often the price of gain.'[11]

Pointers to the Future

The impact of Egan on the CMAC brought about a renewed sense of professional responsibility towards the clients. Training programmes were intensified, updated and subjected to ongoing review. Supervision – the overview of the case by another, usually more experienced, counsellor – was introduced, for beginners at first and later for all practitioners. (Supervision, as a support system for the counsellor, creates what has been termed the 'therapeutic triad'[12] of client/counsellor/supervisor, and is regarded as the best safeguard against what Egan has called the 'shadowy side' of counselling, where the counsellor's own needs and vulnerability intervene in the process.)

Counselling as a therapy to relieve stress is now a growth industry. Egan is only one of numerous authorities in the field and there is a veritable library of literature on the subject. University courses are available. Counselling authorities have evolved, with provision for enrolment and accreditation depending on basic qualifications and adequate work levels, pointing to a future in which a recognised technical qualification will be a requirement to practise.

However, any proposal to require technical qualifications for marriage counselling in Britain and Ireland must have regard to the fact that the main existing agencies, including the CMAC, are voluntary bodies. In 1968 the Seebohm Committee, which reviewed local authority personal social services in Britain, recognised that voluntary bodies had a special role in the care of the family, especially in developing new initiatives. It is a basic requirement for voluntary marriage counsellors in Britain and Ireland that, before they are accepted for training, they have been judged by an exhaustive selection process to possess the essential personal qualities and the disposition for counselling. In other words, while technical qualifications and skills training are essential, it is the counsellor's personal qualities and level of awareness of self which are paramount.

Does Helping Help?

While all the available evidence indicates that counselling invariably produces a degree of relief in the short term, there is however a lingering question as to whether helping really does produce lasting results. The fact is that ever-increasing numbers are availing of counselling, not least those with marital problems. We leave the last word with Egan: '... in the end clients can choose whether to live more effectively or not. Of course the truth is that many clients, because of their interaction with helpers, are not only in a better position to manage the ups and downs of their lives, but actually do so.'[13]

Bernard Leo Cawley KCSG

Born 25 August 1921 within the sound of Bow Bells in London, Bernard Cawley joined the Civil Service in 1939 and, excluding war service, remained there until he retired with the rank of Assistant Secretary to take the post of Chief Executive of the CMAC in 1982. In the war he served in the RAF as a pilot of Liberators in Coastal and, later, Transport Commands when he became familiar with RAF stations at Aldergrove, Ballykelly and Limavady. In the CMAC he served as a counsellor from 1955 to 1987 in four centres, acting at different times as secretary, vice-chairman, chairman and diocesan chairman. He was the first non-medical editor of the *Bulletin* 1971-1982 and a member of the National Executive Committee 1971-1981. A strong advocate of co-operation between counselling organisations, he had a particular attachment to CMAC Ireland where he was a regular and popular visitor to CMAC functions (using the opportunity to acquire a comprehensive knowledge of Irish golf courses). Bernard, twice married and twice widowed, retired as Chief Executive in 1987 and was awarded the KSG in 1987 for his services to the CMAC, raised to KCSG in 1992 for his work with the Cardinal Hume Centre for young people at risk, including a period as Director from 1988 until 1992.

CHAPTER 20

The CMAC and Pre-Marriage Courses

A Church Requirement

A Catholic proposing to marry in the church in North America, Australia, Britain, Ireland, or indeed anywhere in the English-speaking world today, will almost certainly be asked to attend a marriage preparation course. Virtually all of the 175 dioceses in the USA have policies requiring some form of marriage preparation as have those in Britain and in Ireland. Since 1991, the bishops have required the priest to 'ensure that preparation for marriage will have taken place ... The Code (of Canon Law) envisages the provision of marriage preparation by people of proven experience and skill, which in Ireland means a pre-marriage course under the aegis of the CMAC (set up by the bishops for the purpose) or a similar course of instruction.'[1]

The practice of Catholic bishops in recent years to encourage 'proximate preparation for marriage' is affirmed by Pope John Paul II in his letter of 1981, *On the Family:* 'The church must therefore promote better and more intensive programmes of marriage preparation, in order to eliminate as far as possible the difficulties that many married couples find themselves in, and even more in order to favour positively the establishing and maturing of successful marriages.'[2]

Many people would consider that the few short sessions of a pre-marriage course are hardly an adequate response to the Holy Father's instructions. A more lengthy and comprehensive programme is indicated; one beginning in school and extending to the post-marriage years. Nevertheless, it is widely accepted that the preparation courses have the potential to make a valuable, if necessarily limited, contribution towards more successful marriages.

Origins of Pre-Marriage Courses

Marriage preparation courses, 'one of the oldest forms of organised ministry to families', is traced back to Chicago in 1946.[3] The first CMAC courses were delivered in London to British Army personnel in March 1948. (M 89) Major Graham Graham-Green, founder of the CMAC in 1946, records 'it was obvious that prevention was much better than cure; that whilst the immediate necessity was to mend marriages, we must proceed with courses on preparation for marriage.'[4] With the approval of Brigadier Trappes-Lomax, 'a well known Catholic', an experimental course was put on for army personnel. 'The first day of the course went badly but overnight Brigadier Frere and I reorganised the syllabus and by the end of the week it was an outstanding success. Two further courses were run for the army and these were followed by instruction for engaged couples generally.'[5]

Since that time, the CMAC has become the recognised source of marriage preparation courses for Catholics in Britain and, from the founding of the first Catholic marriage counselling centre in Belfast in 1962, in Ireland. Marriage preparation courses were, however, not uncommon in Ireland before the advent of the CMAC. The Catholic Social Welfare Bureau ran courses in Dublin from as early as 1958 as did some of the religious orders in the city. A number of Irish CMAC centres owe their origin to the updating of existing marriage preparation courses; for example, Waterford in 1967 and Dundalk in 1973. The Dundalk courses were established by the late Cardinal Conway in the 1960s when he was Assistant Bishop of Armagh and they were still running when the new CMAC centre took over in 1973.

Absence of Research

It is a remarkable fact that while, since their inception, literally thousands of CMAC marriage preparation courses have taken place in Britain and in Ireland, no research has been done to test their effectiveness in terms of contributing to more satisfactory or more stable marriages. The fact that the Irish hierarchy has always been in favour of such courses, and made them mandatory in 1991, implies a certain confidence in their worth. The bishops have not, however, laid down specific requirements as to the objectives and content of the courses, leaving it to the counsellors

to devise what they consider appropriate. A hint of the minimum expected by the bishops is given in the Pastoral
Guidelines: 'in cases where, for whatever reason, the person
does not attend a pre-marriage course, the priest has the obligation of giving instruction on matters essential to an adult understanding of Christian marriage, including the sacramental (can.
1063.2).'

There is therefore an obvious presumption on the part of the
bishops that attendance at a marriage preparation course will result, at least, in 'an adult understanding of Christian marriage
including the sacramental'. The absence of specific guidelines
from the bishops has, however, led to a certain ambivalence at
CMAC centres as to what they are expected to achieve and, consequently, a wide variation in the standards of the courses offered. In the words of one commentator, 'While it is indeed true
that the churches are the main providers of that which exists,
what is provided is extremely patchy and variable.'[6] Research
done in Canada and the USA, based largely on the reaction of
those who have attended, shows a generally favourable reaction
amongst the 'consumers', with the inevitable minority at the extreme ends of the spectrum – from those who thought the courses
one of the best forms of pastoral ministry in the church, to the
lady who said 'I think it was a complete waste of time – a torture
you must endure in order to be married by the church.'[7]

Exceptional Skills Required
Participants in CMAC marriage preparation courses are unlike
the students in a school classroom or university lecture hall.
Typically, there is a wide mixture of ages, of social backgrounds,
of educational qualifications and of interest in the course and,
correspondingly, a wide variation in the capacity to respond to a
learning process. To impart a new and deeper appreciation of
marriage to such a diverse group calls for more subtle teaching
methods than the didactic 'talk and chalk' approach. It is a task
for highly-trained counsellors with group-facilitation skills and
a capacity to extend their counselling skills into the educational
area.[8]

The Problem with Sex
The first CMAC marriage preparation course for civilians was
given in Luton in 1949. (M 89) There was much agonising in the
NEC as 'to what extent the physical side should be discussed before mixed audiences', with the conclusion that there should be
one lecture for the sexes separately and two for them together. It
also said that 'in none of these is sex instruction to be given.
There is a big difference between sex instruction and sex education.' The final conclusion was that 'to be on the safe side' the
matter should be referred to one of the ecclesiastical advisors,
Canon Denning, who approved the syllabus (as had Cardinal
Griffin). Marshall records that a 'senior army chaplain still had
lingering doubts about the propriety about what was proposed
which he expressed in a letter ... It was therefore decided to establish an education subcommittee (the first in the CMAC) to
monitor the work ... The whole episode illustrates the difficulty
encountered in dealing with sexual matters in those days and
the need constantly to refer to ecclesiastical authorities "to be on
the safe side".' (M 89)

Growth and Development
The development of the programmes owed much to Fr Frank
Handley, who joined CMAC as Head of Training in 1959, and
who ran the courses for the next fourteen years. Marshall's outline of the courses is worth recording because, as noted above, it
mirrors what was occurring in the Irish centres at that time. (The
Irish centres were serviced by CMAC headquarters in London
until 'independence' in 1975.)

Marshall writes: 'With the growth in the centres in the 1950s,
the number of engaged couples' courses run by CMAC nation-
wide increased. A few were of the one-day (usually Sunday)
type; these were discouraged as not providing an opportunity
for a relationship to be built up between the course leaders and
the couples. Most were in the form of weekly sessions of six or
eight weeks. The format was a talk followed by questions followed by a chat over tea and biscuits. The usual subjects were
the sacrament, budgeting, housing, sex, parenthood, and getting
on together; some courses devoted a special session to the 'wedding'. Initially these were largely information-giving sessions

but gradually increasing emphasis was placed on relationships. The course leaders were encouraged to attend every session so that they would get to know the couples and the couples them, enabling them to open up on matters that they would not wish to raise at question time.

'The session on sex was given by a doctor, one to the young men and one to the young women. The need for separation was much debated; on the one hand, it was argued, that if a couple were to share a sex life together, they should learn about it together, so that each would know what the other knew; the contrary argument was that though it might be all right for a couple to learn together, it was not appropriate for them to be learning with somebody else. Eventually the session was given jointly but this owed more to a general change in attitude towards sex in society than to new insights in the CMAC.' (M 90)

The Impact of the CMAC

The CMAC must get credit for responding to social changes and the developing insights into the effectiveness of pre-marriage courses by constantly upgrading the course presentation. In Ireland, prior to the CMAC era, the premarriage courses were, in Marshall's words, basically 'information-giving' sessions with the couples (occasionally as many as thirty) passively attentive as various specialists addressed them from a rostrum in the parish hall. In the beginning this pattern was followed by the new centres in Ireland except that, the courses being more frequent, the attendance was not so large. In those days, counsellors were selected for either remedial counselling or educational counselling. By the mid-1960s, under the influence of the tutors trained in Britain, the pattern began to change towards more group discussion led by the education counsellors. Tony Campbell, one of the first Irish tutors, and his wife Mairéad, an educational counsellor, are remembered for running a very lively course in Newry in 1968 (the centre's second year of operation) using model situations for case discussion. The Campbells' principle was 'minimum input from the counsellors and maximum from the couples'.[9]

It was the beginning of a general trend away from information-giving towards an emphasis on the couple's relationship with each other. The employment of visiting specialists gave way to sessions designed to help the couples get to know one another by adopting a more counselling approach in small groups. In Brian Howlett's words: 'The "experts" were tactfully pensioned off and, under our group leadership, the engaged couples sought, by talking with us and among themselves, to understand and re-examine their own attitudes and values in the areas of sex, money, marital roles, religion, male and female needs, fertility control and so forth.'[10] Fr Peter Rudman, chief executive of CMAC and head of external courses in Britain (1976-1982), 'identified five areas in marriage preparation in which a counselling approach would be appropriate: motivation for marriage, expectations, degree of tolerance or frustration, understanding of self and of partner, and ability to assume responsibility for one's actions.' (M 91)

A further refinement, developed in the early 1980s, was the 'couple-centred' exercises based on the work of an American, Dr David Rolfe. Rolfe had done some research in the USA and found, as most people suspected, that the information-giving sessions were not only unpopular but made little or no impact. He devised simple exercises by which each couple separately completed a questionnaire which they then compared, discovering in the process their differing attitudes and values, which they discussed, firstly together and then in small groups.[11] This couple-focused system did much to resolve the problem of dealing in groups with couples from different backgrounds. Brian Howlett comments on this methodology: 'The method used of involving couples in dealing with direct questions has some very pertinent benefits: it structures information in a way that can be handled by the couple; it allows them to get involved at their own level and in concrete terms; it enables them to become aware of events or behaviour which they have taken for granted or have developed beneath the level of their awareness, and encourages them to look at such events or behaviour differently and to think unthinkable thoughts about what is happening in their lives.'[12]

Resistance to Change
The problem with such 'counselling-based' courses was the de-

mand they made on the counsellors in terms of detailed preparation and skilled delivery. The 'information-giving' courses
were much less demanding in this respect and survived for this
and other reasons, depending largely on the attitudes and the
energy of those at the centre, not least the centre priest. Not all
centres were willing to disturb an established system that gave
no problems. Some specialists with a gift for public speaking so
enjoyed their role that they were hard to dislodge.[13] In the background too were clergy of the old school who had a problem
with the church fostering discussion in groups where matters
contrary to church teaching might be upheld. They favoured information-giving by reliable people as being more consistent
with the role of the 'teaching church'. For such reasons there
were still a few centres in Ireland running old-style courses as
'talks for engaged couples' into the 1990s.

New Blood – New Ideas
The single most effective element of change was the reform of
the counsellors' basic training course from 1978. Counsellors
who had more intensive training, including training in group
leadership, made an immediate impact in the centres, so much
so that there were occasionally tensions between the newcomers
and their settled colleagues resistant to new methods. In at least
one centre the problem was temporarily resolved by running
two types of pre-marriage courses alternately, one by the 'modernists' and one by the 'traditionalists'. Eventually, as the traditionalists departed the scene, the 'modernists' prevailed!

A feature of the more progressive centres was the constant
preoccupation with re-assessment of the courses. 'Inquests'
were held at the end of every course to review the strengths and
weaknesses. Written questionnaires were found to be unsatis-
factory in that couples were reluctant to criticise or complain.[14]
Visual aids and other devices to provide discussion topics were
gradually discarded as obstructions to establishing the counsel-
lor-couple relationship vital to facilitate the learning process.
The trouble was that there was still need for the 'facilitating' approach to be balanced with 'information-giving'. Marshall
found that 'giving of information was dropped. In some centres
this was carried to such a degree that one couple was moved to

write to the chairman of the executive committee complaining that, at a course they had attended, birth regulation was never even mentioned.' (M 91/2) Clearly too the subject of marriage as a sacrament called for an input, normally by the centre priest.

The Time Factor and Other Considerations

Marshall refers to the importance of establishing a relationship between the couples and those delivering the course and the limitation of one-day courses in this regard. (M 90) Weekly sessions, on the other hand, give couples a space to absorb the experience and to discuss between themselves the matters raised. Recent American research found that the 'perceived value is lowest for respondents who had only one session, rises continually for those who had up to eight to nine sessions, and then diminishes for those who had more than nine sessions.'[15] The same American study found also that the 'perceived value' of the course is strongest in the early years of marriage and fades as the years go on. The presence of a priest at the courses was much appreciated. It also found that 'the mandatory nature of marriage preparation in the Catholic Church does not appear to get in the way of participants finding value in it.' The CMAC in Britain and in Ireland had a different experience – particularly in the first years – when some couples, indignant at this new condition for marriage, disrupted the courses. Now, as the church law is more widely known and accepted, there are fewer problems, though the presence of unwilling conscripts can still produce a 'chill factor', especially at the opening session.

Setting Goals

Whilst marriage preparation courses have obvious limitations, they clearly have a potential for contributing to better marriages provided the courses are delivered with wisdom and skill. The courses are increasingly the subject of study by agencies concerned with family welfare, in order to improve their effectiveness and identify the appropriate means to develop in each couple 'a developing awareness of what is involved in creating and recreating the foundation for two people to become one flesh yet remain separate persons. Marriage education should help the couple to view marriage not as a status to be achieved but as a commitment to continual growth and change.'[16] In Ireland, Family Caring Trust has synthesised the basic requirements into a number of achievable goals, which include: helping couples to shed enough baggage to be able to embark on a new phase in their relationship; teaching them to cope with changing family relationships; teaching them communication skills and how to deal with conflict; encouraging them to make a conscious decision to give time to their relationship; and to make them aware that help is available when problems arise. 'This is an ideal. It will not be realised fully and is not meant to overawe people planning marriage education. But it may be useful to have an overview like this in the back of our minds for it can bring clarity and a sense of direction to the task ahead.'[17]

These developments and insights testify to ever increasing demands on those who deliver pre-marriage courses in terms of commitment and of counselling and teaching skills, and point to the probability that the church's marriage counselling service will eventually engage a corps of paid part-time professionals to design and conduct pre-marriage courses with trained voluntary counsellors acting in a supporting role.

CHAPTER 21

The NFP Service

A Separate Service

Instruction in fertility awareness as the basis of family planning by natural methods (which became known as NFP) is now an integral component of Accord's marriage counselling service. Training in fertility awareness is included in the basic training of counsellors going into the 'Marriage Care' division of the service, and from these a number will specialise in face-to-face counselling of couples seeking advice.

This is in contrast to the early years of the CMAC when the service was offered under three discrete branches – remedial, educational and medical. These groups tended to operate independently, especially the medical section. The doctors, and later the nurses who assisted them, met separately in their centres and at medical conferences. The doctors were available to help with any medically-related marriage problems and any remedial work in the sexual area. (In the pre-marriage courses a doctor would take the session on sexuality behind closed doors and drawn blinds!) The main area of their work, however, was advising on NFP which in those first years was exclusively in the doctors' domain.

This is not remarkable, as it was the determination of Catholic doctors to have a family planning service available to Catholics that resulted in the launching of the CMAC in Ireland[1] and in the development of the CMAC medical service in Britain. Marshall relates how the insistence of Birmingham doctors led to the establishment of a national medical committee: 'It was Dr Ruth Sanderson from Glasgow who, in 1952, visited headquarters to seek advice on how to secure the establishment of a centre in the west of Scotland. It was continued pressure from the Catholic doctors in Belfast, especially Dr Raymond Magill, which forced reluctant ecclesiastical authorities to open the first Irish centre in that city in 1962.' (M 101)

Early Attitudes

Natural family planning is based essentially on a knowledge of human fertility. It was not until 1929/30 that two research workers, Herman Knaus in Austria and Kynsaku Ogino in Japan, independently established that ovulation occurs about 14 days before the onset of the next period. Their discovery gave rise to control of fertility by the calendar or Ogino/ Knaus method and, for the first time, provided an acceptable means of birth control for Catholics. The church held contraception by mechanical or chemical means as always morally sinful.[2] Contraception by abstinence was held not sinful 'if it is agreed by both spouses and there is sufficient reason for its use.'[3]

Marshall recalls the prevailing attitude in Britain in the early days of the CMAC when 'family planning or birth regulation were dirty words in Catholic circles. Parents were urged to 'trust in God'; large families were hailed as a sign of sanctity; talking to engaged couples about NFP was considered wrong; it was only in extreme circumstances that people should seek to regulate the size of their family even by legitimate means ... Counsellors in London were instructed that they should only refer a couple to a medical advisor for NFP instruction if they were married, had at least two children and had written permission from their parish priest ... In 1956 it was felt necessary to seek approval from Cardinal Griffin for research to be carried out in NFP; this was given.' (M 103)

This antipathy to family planning was largely due to a reaction to Marie Stopes' promotion of contraception by artificial means as a benefit to marriage and to save women from the physical strain of excessive childbearing. Her first book, *Married Love*, was published in 1918, and she opened Britain's first birth control clinic in Holloway, London, in 1921. Marie Stopes was actually a distinguished botanist.[4] The failure of her first marriage in 1916 turned her mind to marriage problems. To the Catholic Church her book and clinics were largely regarded as the work of the devil and indeed, according to Dr Raymond Magill, the medical profession was for many years reluctant to be associated with her campaign.[5]

Vatican Roulette

All methods of contraception (other than sterilisation), including the most 'reliable' of the artificial methods, are subject to failure for various reasons, including human mismanagement. In this respect, the calendar method proved to be notoriously risky. The Ogina/Knaus formula included one innocent looking little word, 'before', which caused all the difficulty. Ovulation, it said, occurs 14 days before the onset of the next menstruation. Unfortunately predicting the onset of the next menstruation has always proved to be a hazardous business. Even the most 'regular' healthy woman is subject to the occasional variation in ovulation, two or three days either way, not to mention the effect of illness, sudden stress or medication, and of course there are those whose monthly periods are highly irregular. When all the possibilities are taken into consideration the number of 'safe' days are whittled down to about four before and four after the onset of a period. Naturally, risks were taken and consequently there was a high 'failure' rate so that the method became known cynically as 'Vatican Roulette'!

The Breakthrough

In 1959 an important refinement of the calendar method greatly advanced its reliability. This was the basal body temperature method (BBT) developed by Dutch gynaecologist Dr J G H Holt. Dr John Marshall went with Fr O'Leary to visit Dr Holt, who was enthusiastic about his discovery. Marshall describes how the doctor eagerly spread his large display charts on the floor of the departure lounge at Schipol Airport, quite indifferent to the astonishment of the bystanders. (M 104) The basis of the BBT was the abrupt and measurable rise in body temperature at ovulation which persisted until the next period. The method 'was quickly adopted as the standard method of NFP taught in the CMAC; special charts were designed, instructions printed and arrangements for the supply of thermometers made. With the later recognition of the significant changes in the cervical mucus by Drs John and Evelyn Billings, in Australia, this was added to the BBT in what was called the mucothermic or symptothermic[6] method.' (M 104)

Professor Marshall is recognised as the one who led the promotion of the BBT method and who, through scientific research published in medical journals, established the validity of the method in the secular world. Marshall describes how the strength of the CMAC in the field of NFP was based on its own research. It was the main plank in the CMAC's response to the propaganda of the Family Planning Association which was dismissive of NFP. For this reason too, CMAC was unique among organisations promoting NFP in its insistence that instruction be given by doctors. A study of the calendar method commenced in January 1958, started by Dr Anthony Coady and Dr Joan May and completed by Dr Jack Dominian and Dr Michael Moore when Dr Coady went abroad. It 'showed a pregnancy rate of 9.4 per 100 women per year, comparable to that of the condom and diaphragm, which were the methods in general use at the time ... The importance of the research was formally recognised by the national medical committee in 1962 when it established a research committee with Dr Jack Dominian, Dr John Marshall and Mr Bernard Parker FRCOG, a gynaecologist from the Birmingham centre, as members.' In 1965 a four-year grant from the Population Council enabled work on no less than twelve major research projects, 'the results being published in prestigious, peer-reviewed medical journals. Among these were the first field trials of the BBT method of regulating births ...' (M 104-5)

NFP in Ireland

The BBT method of fertility awareness was well-established in Britain by the time the first Catholic marriage counselling centre in Ireland opened in Belfast in 1962. By the time Dublin and Armagh came on board to make a total of 11 centres in Ireland, each centre had its panel of doctors and trained nurses to advise on NFP. Fate took a hand when the method came to the notice of one who was to play a major role in the promotion of NFP in Ireland. This was Dr Esther Bradley who lived with her dentist husband, Alex, and young family near Lifford in Co Donegal. Esther elected to be a 'homemaker' with occasional stints as locum for local doctors. One day in 1966 a priest friend handed her John Marshall's book on NFP saying, 'take a look at this and tell me what you think if it.' She was immediately interested and set up some trials among her friends. Some time later she attended a CMAC medical conference in England, her first contact with CMAC, and from then became a convinced convert. In 1971 she and Alex were selected as CMAC counsellors for the adjacent diocese of Raphoe and did the basic training course, transferring later to their own diocese of Derry when the first centre opened there in 1973. Esther later trained with the first tutors trained in Ireland in Bellinter in 1976.

Dr Bradley had special gifts as a communicator which brought her into prominence in Ireland and later on the world stage. Attractive, humorous and coherent, she had a natural stage presence. Her two main strengths as a speaker were firstly, her manifest sincerity and her obvious personal conviction that the management of fertility by natural methods was not only an effective way of planned parenthood but the key to an enriched relationship for the couple, and secondly, as a good counsellor, her non-directive attitude. She preferred to address the subject as 'fertility awareness' rather than as NFP, since fertility awareness was equally important for those wanting a baby and, in any event, the management of their fertility was ultimately a matter for each couple to decide.

Humanae Vitae, the encyclical letter of Pope Paul VI in 1968 which condemned all artificial forms of contraception, including the pill, gave the NFP service a higher priority in the CMAC activities. By 1976 (Fr Kennedy's first year as director in Ireland) Marshall writes, 'the battle for the acceptance of the validity of NFP had been won and so CMAC felt able to introduce lay-teachers into the NFP programme.' (M 106) Training courses were set up including one at the Oxford centre which medical and other staff from the local services attended. This was a significant development in that the delivery of the service was moving out of the domain of the doctors to that of the 'lay' counsellors.

When he arrived as National Director at the end of 1975, Fr Kennedy had no reservations about the importance of the NFP service and the need to deliver the service at a professional level. He soon recruited Dr Bradley to head the NFP service and had her take tutor training in 1976, along with Mary Higgins, a midwife who had been a teacher of NFP in the Cork centre. In September of that year Dr Bradley attended a conference in

Vienna. In the chair was the French Canadian Dr Claude Lanctot who was promoting the organisation of which he was Director General, the 'International Federation For Family Life Promotion' (IFFLP), with which Dr Bradley was to be closely associated in the following years. Meanwhile Mary Higgins met Dr Anna Flynn, a Birmingham obstetrician who was active in the IFFLP and also involved in a WHO research project testing educational materials for NFP in Canada, Chile, Korea, Kenya, the Phillipines and Great Britain. Dr Flynn invited Mary to join the British project team. While in Birmingham, Mary Higgins and Helen Scott (another member of the project team) organised a four-week NFP training course for people from anglophone African countries. Following this experience, Mary spent some months of each year from 1979 to 1984 working as an IFFLP consultant and became acquainted with leading figures in NFP on the world stage.

The International Federation of Family Life Promotion
The IFFLP was incorporated in Washington DC on 16 September 1974. Dr Marshall records that it grew from contacts between the CMAC and visitors to the International Congress of Catholic doctors in London in 1962, which gave rise to the consideration of an international organisation concerned with natural family planning, and which eventually resulted in the founding of the IFFLP. The first meeting of the organisation was held in Washington in August 1974. Amongst the twenty-two delegates from thirteen countries attending were Fr O'Leary and Dr John O'Keefe of the English CMAC, which, according to Marshall: 'exercised a major influence in the development of the organisation. Despite its title some members saw it as being exclusively devoted to NFP; some even put forward the view that it was through the fertility awareness involved in NFP that the whole of the marriage relationship was built up. This was a view that CMAC did not share, believing that there was more to the marriage relationship than fertility awareness.' (M 105)

Exclusive devotion to NFP is in fact enshrined in the IFFLP constitution. In the six sub-clauses to the Third Article, which sets out the purposes of the organisation, every one relates to the promotion of 'natural family planning'. The essential ethos of the organisation is set out in paragraphs six and seven of the Appendix. 'In this context (of family values as stated in the foregoing five paragraphs) natural family planning is defined as a dialogue leading to responsible parenthood based on an educated awareness and acceptance of the cyclic phases of fertility and infertility, and loving abstinence in married life becomes basic to this dialogue.' (These sentiments are resonant of *Humanae Vitae*, Section 21.) Paragraph seven continues: 'The International Federation For Family Life Promotion respects and accepts spiritual values from whatever source, which may deepen the understanding and sustain the purpose of a person or a couple.'

It was clearly Fr Kennedy's policy to have the CMAC Ireland associated with the IFFLP. In 1977 Dr Bradley accompanied Professor John Bonnar and Dr Anna Flynn[7] to two meetings on NFP under the auspices of the World Health Organisation,[8] the initial meeting in Geneva in February and the final meeting at Rockwell College in April, in preparation for a WHO trial of the ovulation method of NFP involving five centres – Manila, San Miguel, Dublin, Auckland and Bangalore – which was completed in 1981. In June of 1977 Dr Bradley participated with Professor Bonnar and Dr Flynn in the first international conference of the IFFLP in Cali, Columbia, and later played a prominent part in the second international conference which was hosted by CMAC Ireland in Bellinter in October 1980. In February 1978 Dr Bradley had been to the first international conference in Melbourne on the Billings ovulation method. Mary Higgins, as we have seen, had made her own way into the IFFLP organisation. In April 1981 Dr Bradley and Mary Higgins formed a team of consultants with Dr Flynn to conduct workshops for NFP trainers in Lusaka and Nairobi. The CMAC Ireland continued to send delegates to IFFLP conferences. Between 1983 and 1987 Fr Kennedy, Fr Tony King, Mary Higgins and Dorothy Scally were among those who attended. This close involvement with IFFLP[9] obviously raised the profile of CMAC Ireland on the international stage.

Government Promotion of NFP
In 1978 political developments in the South had a significant impact on the expansion of the NFP service in the CMAC. Charlie Haughey, the Minister of Health, was drafting his Family

Planning Act of 1979. His proposal to permit the sale of contraceptives to married couples had to be balanced with government support for natural methods (his famous 'Irish solution to
an Irish problem'!) In collaboration with the WHO, he organised
an International Seminar on Natural Methods of Family
Planning in the Marine Hotel, Dun Laoghaire, on 8 and 9
October 1979 to which he invited Dr Bradley as a speaker. Then,
in consultation with the Irish bishops, he offered a block grant
towards the development of an NFP service to be delivered by
the CMAC. For better or worse, the CMAC had become involved in a government scheme for the provision of family planning in the South! Mr Haughey was a very wily politician.

In June 1981 Fr Kennedy, in fulfilment of a commitment to
government, appointed Dr Bradley Head of CMAC Medical
Services for a three-year period and appointed Mary Higgins
and Dorothy Scally as NFP consultants for a similar period.
Apparently the government's foundation grant could only
stretch to the consultants' salaries for three years.[10] Dr Bradley
agreed to work on a voluntary basis. The task of this team was to
promote NFP and train lay people as instructors. Only counsellors selected for NFP were offered training in accordance with
CMAC Ireland policy that (unless in exceptional circumstances)
all CMAC services be delivered only by counsellors who had
undergone selection and basic training. Furthermore, it was
now accepted, thanks to the insights of Dorothy Scally and
others, that the effective delivery of NFP on a face-to-face basis
required a degree of counselling skills in addition to technical
knowledge.

Dorothy Scally was exceptional as the member of the NFP
team with no medical background. Her first acquaintance with
NFP was at a course for engaged couples which led to a fascina-
tion with the whole subject of fertility and the potential of fertility
awareness to enrich the marriage relationship. In this regard she
saw the strictly pedagogic approach as inadequate, and developed a philosophy of NFP counselling on the Rogerian principles of regard and respect for the couple and of the role of the
counsellor in enabling them to discover in NFP the source of an
enhanced togetherness in their marriage. Dorothy's exceptional
intellect and her communication skills, verbally and in writing,

marked her for rapid promotion from NFP teacher at the Harcourt Street centre of the CMAC to the first NFP 'tutor body' in Ireland and eventually to central office as NFP consultant.

Product
The first assignment of the team was to conduct a series of meetings countrywide, directed towards clergy, doctors, nurses and other key personnel, that would promote NFP as a practical and reliable method of birth control. It proved an exhausting job, physically and mentally, involving endless miles of travel and late hours. Dr Bradley reckons that she motored some 20,000 miles a year on this campaign, met every bishop in Ireland and most of the clergy, as well as doctors, hospital matrons, nursing staff, social workers and a host of others concerned with family welfare. It was a hectic time, exhausting but also exhilarating for herself and her two assistants. There were inevitably the occasional 'protesters' – including doctors – voicing their scepticism of the philosophy of NFP in general and of *Humanae Vitae* in particular. On the other hand there were the rewards of the social side: meeting counsellors from the various centres and their friends, lots of entertainment and much encouraging approbation.

Dr Bradley retired in 1984 at the end of her three year 'contract' and was not replaced. Her elegant unassuming style added lustre to the team at central office; her ready smile and her willingness to help personified the best qualities of doctor and counsellor and set the highest standard of professionalism for the CMAC.

The training programme fell to two consultants, both highly competent and dedicated to the work. Dorothy Scally, based in Dublin, was responsible for the Dublin area, and Mary Higgins, based in Galway, had responsibility for the rest of Ireland. Mary's energy was legendary. She typically travelled the length and breadth of Ireland full of enthusiasm for her job. As the number of trained counsellors increased the pressure eased somewhat. They were working themselves out of a job! Eventually one post fell victim to financial constraints and Mary departed in 1985 to resume her career as a midwife in a Cork hospital. Dorothy Scally remained as professional head of NFP until her resignation in 1993 and was succeeded by Ursula Peelo.

In the mid 1980s the NFP service moved further into the mainstream of the CMAC activities. The basic training course was upgraded to consist of 'core training', taken by all new entrants, followed by specialised training (depending on the needs of the centre), either remedial counselling or 'marriage care' counselling which incorporates training in the delivery of pre-marriage courses including sessions on fertility awareness and NFP.

The demand for NFP counselling remains surprisingly steady. For many couples, within and without the Catholic community, it is the preferred way of managing their fertility. Since 1996, kits that offer more accurate predictions of fertility awareness by monitoring hormonal changes, have come onto the commercial market. While NFP is commonly associated with birth prevention, there are also couples who seek information in the hope of achieving a pregnancy. Another common, and unfounded, belief is that all young adults have a basic scientific knowledge of human fertility. Accord marriage care counsellors report that a surprising number attending pre-marriage courses have little or no knowledge of the connection between the menstrual cycle and fertility, other than 'street-wisdom' that intercourse is liable to lead to a pregnancy.

CHAPTER 22

The CMAC Schools Service

The Authority of the Church

'Children and young people should be helped to develop harmoniously their physical, moral and intellectual qualities ... As they grow older they should receive a positive and prudent education in matters relating to sex ... Children and young people have the right to be stimulated to make sound moral judgements based on a well-formed conscience and to put them into practice with a sense of personal commitment.'[1]

The schools programme in Ireland was the CMAC's implementation of this directive from the Second Vatican Council (1962-65). The service expanded with the growth in the number of centres throughout the 1960s and 70s and was affirmed by the Irish bishops from their Episcopal Conference in Mulrany in 1974, when they recommended 'a strong liaison between the post primary schools and CMAC in the area of educating for life and particularly for marriage.'[2]

The Belfast centre made history, not only by being the first Catholic marriage counselling centre in Ireland, but also by anticipating the Vatican II document and initiating the first such programmes in secondary schools as part of their 'educational counselling' service. Unfortunately, almost as soon as the service was well established, the schools programme was suspended by the priest director for reasons unknown, and never resumed.[3] A number of the counsellors involved were, however, engaged by the more progressive schools as 'relationships' teachers, and had the satisfaction of seeing the subject become the basis of a new examination subject for the Certificate in Secondary Education (now General Certificate in Secondary Education) in the North.

The Wider Context

From the outset it was evident that the original objective of imparting 'positive and prudent information in matters relating to sex' could best be done in the context of education in human relationships, including relationships with the opposite sex. So the programmes became known as 'education for personal relationships' (EPR). Working with small groups of young people convinced counsellors that the most secure basis for personal decision-making and responsibility ('sound moral judgements') was a sense of self-worth and self-respect. Pupils taking part were seen to grow in self-confidence as they practised identifiable and teachable skills in relating, such as self awareness, 'clarifying', 'reflecting back' and 'challenging'. Good group leadership ensured that relationships were 'caught as well as taught'.

Parents in Need

Since nothing could be done without the consent and the co-operation of the parents, the schools invited parents to meetings which teachers also attended. These meetings were a revelation. The parents, brought up in a world where matters of sexuality were never mentioned or discussed, had found themselves having to answer questions from their children prompted by television programmes, magazine articles and other such sources dealing with procreation and sexuality.[4] The first experience of the counsellors at parents' meetings was of the overwhelming demand for help in this area. How were they to deal with these awkward questions? When and how were they to give information to small children? What language were they to use? How much information should they give to girls (and boys) approaching puberty? Harrowing tales were heard of mothers who as girls had had no warning of, or help to deal with, the onset of menstruation. Others had gone to hospital to have their first baby wondering where the baby came out. Small booklets, designed to provide appropriate information for children of varying ages, were eagerly snapped up by the parents as aids to finding a vocabulary and the ability to communicate with their children. It was in fact the parents themselves who were most immediately in need of sex education!

The enthusiasm of the parents for schools programmes and

for parents' meetings was a tremendous reassurance to the counsellors in their new venture, and to those school principals who had become convinced that schools should be doing something to counter non-Christian influences from the world outside. They welcomed into the classrooms people with expertise in handling what they perceived as 'difficult topics', and with skills in group leadership.

In the Classrooms
The group setting was particularly appropriate to relationships education as it provided for the application of counselling principles at the sensitive stage when attitudes to sexuality were forming. 'As with one-to-one counselling, the tools the counsellor uses are listening, reflecting back, reflective discussion. The members will learn about themselves in a 'safe' situation. The counsellor sets the tone for the whole group.'[5] The subject ranged over the world of young people: school and home, the family in society, the impact of social problems on the family, and of changing roles and behaviour. The courses became known as 'family life studies' or 'education for living', and were very popular with the students.

It soon became evident that the subject could not be dealt with in isolation from other subjects in the curriculum. Teachers of religion, biology, health and physical education were obviously affected and their co-operation was essential. Consideration of the beauty inherent in relationships and sexuality, and the subtleties of the emotions and feelings, touched on the creative arts which was the domain of the teachers of art, music and literature. The subject had therefore a cross-curricular dimension affecting, directly or indirectly, various other teachers in the school whose awareness and support were essential, as indeed were the awareness and the general support of the management and the entire teaching staff.

It was a short step to the inevitable conclusion that 'education for living' should properly be delivered, not by visiting counsellors, but by members of the teaching staff as an integral part of the school curriculum. Occasional visits by counsellors lacked the necessary continuity and for that reason became regarded as counter-productive. The fact that they were marriage counsellors suggested a focus on married love, a distortion which was to give trouble later. Nevertheless, the CMAC had blazed the trail. They had shown the demand for relationships education in schools and had demonstrated the means of delivery. What they now had to offer was a reservoir of skills available to teaching staffs. The time had come to hand over to the educational system.

A Change of Direction
The focus of the CMAC in Britain and in Ireland consequently changed towards encouraging schools to include education for personal relationships in their curricula. Providing resource material and teacher support became the immediate task. In September 1978 the CMAC in London joined with the Westminster Education Commission to produce a handbook, *Education for Personal Relationships,* a curriculum for secondary schools, written by Margaret Grimer with a Foreword by Bishop Konstant of Westminster. A most comprehensive document for its size, it set out in detail the aims and the objectives as well as the methods and the contents of EPR programmes in secondary schools. This was followed in September 1979 by another EPR handbook from the CMAC in London, *Resources For Relationships,* a selection of teaching materials. In Dublin Sheila Campbell, pioneer of relationships education in Belfast and now Head of the CMAC Ireland Schools Service, produced (with the co-operation of the Communications Centre) *Tell Me More,* a set of tapes for teachers of boys and girls of 11 to 16 years, and *Education For Love,* a course for post-primary schools.

The introduction of this new subject into the school curriculum was not simply a matter of providing space for an extra subject, difficult though that might be. Teachers who considered their first responsibility was to achieve good examination results, had to be persuaded of the value of this new venture and that, with appropriate training, they had the abilities to carry out the programmes. The group method raised the novel idea of 'student-centred teaching' in Rogerian terms, not readily acceptable to staff trained in the traditional 'talk and chalk' mode.[6] Parents had to be consulted and approve. Meanwhile there were disturbing sounds of opposition, in Britain and in Ireland, from those who regarded 'sex education' as exclusively the responsibility of parents in the home and not a function of schools. School authorities could not ignore such objections even if they believed them to be unjustified.

EPR on a Rising Tide

Nevertheless, throughout the early 80s, an ever increasing number of secondary schools in Ireland, including Catholic schools, were offering EPR courses in some form. At least one Education Board in the South and the Department of Education in the North were actively encouraging secondary schools to embark on EPR programmes and had guidelines prepared for teachers. In 1985, following the Granard tragedy,[7] there was a clamour in the media for more 'sex education' in schools. In response, the state-sponsored Health Education Bureau (HEB) in the South began to prepare a schools programme. Veritas, a church-sponsored publishing house in Dublin, was directed by the Irish bishops to produce an EPR manual for Catholic teachers. Veritas appointed a working party to carry out the project. The group, which included a number of experienced EPR teachers, soon concluded that the promotion of EPR programmes required not only a teachers' manual but a back-up campaign to promote its adoption in Catholic schools with appropriate resources and ongoing support for the teachers involved. The project was, however, overtaken by events and had a sudden demise.

The Resistance Movement

In the late 70s and early 80s there was a build-up of resistance in the South to proposals for relaxation of the laws prohibiting divorce and the sale of contraceptives and any other proposals seen as favouring a more permissive society. A number of opposing organisations grew up, foremost amongst them a particularly strident group called Family Solidarity which spearheaded a campaign against 'sex education' in Catholic schools. No sooner had the Veritas working party got into action than they received representations from Family Solidarity on the dangers to Catholic children inherent in these programmes (regardless of the fact that this group, chaired by a priest, was acting for the Irish bishops). Their arguments appeared to be based on the assumption that relationships education was a euphemism for a covert introduction of young peoples to the joys of sex, or in their words: 'merely an introduction to the experience of pleasure and a stimulus leading to the loss of serenity – while still in the years of innocence – by opening the way to vice.'[8] According to Family Solidarity, the national media had created the impression that there was an urgent need for sex education in all schools and as a consequence a state programme 'which could only be hostile to Catholic teaching' was being prepared. 'The introduction and wide acceptance of such a state programme would be an unmitigated disaster.' 'Even in Catholic schools, damage has been done by sex education programmes, designed and administered by groups outside the Catholic school system which do not subscribe to Catholic values.' They urged the church to produce a programme immediately which would 'effectively sterilise the HEB one' and 'for purposes of control', to confine the subject to religion class 'even if teachers of religion have to be specially trained for it.'

Aware that these representations were based on a false premise, the working party disregarded them as irrelevant – which proved to be a fatal error. The views of Family Solidarity got an unexpected mandate from none other than Kevin McNamara, the Archbishop of Dublin, on 4 February 1986 when, at a Mass for the reopening of Blackrock College Chapel, he rounded on 'certain educational programmes the effect of which is to weaken the effort of young people to grow in self-discipline and to undermine a certain essential reticence, modesty and sense of reverence.' Predictably the media had a field day, the *Irish Independent's* headline, 'Liberal Approach to Sex Slated by Archbishop' being typical.

The archbishop had indicated that he intended to have a 'book' produced under his direction for teachers' guidance and therefore was withdrawing his support for the Veritas project, which then closed down. The HEB programme found few takers and disappeared when the HEB itself was disbanded by government as an economy measure. In 1986 the new director of the CMAC closed down the schools service on the grounds that the organisation lacked sufficient resources. *Love Matters*, the book written by Francis Mc Crickard for the archbishop, appeared in

1987 and was highly commended. Veritas sold out the first edition of 10,000 copies but it was not reprinted. Veritas also produced two accompanying videos, one by Francis McCrickard
and one by Angela McNamara.

Neither the book nor the videos could undo the setback to
EPR programmes in Catholic secondary schools following the
archbishop's intervention, particularly in the South. In the
North the Department of Education quietly continued to promote EPR programmes which some Catholic schools adopted.
Eleven years later in 1997 an EPR programme was introduced
by the Education Department in the South, and, notwithstand-
ing the inevitable voices of opposition, received the support of
the Irish bishops. That 'unmitigated disaster' which Family
Solidarity had so bitterly opposed in 1985 had come to pass –
programmes for relationships education exclusively in the
hands of the secular authorities.

Postscript
The work of the CMAC counsellors in promoting EPR was essentially pioneering work in terms of curricular development in
the Catholic educational system. More significantly it had as its
ethos a respect for traditional family values and was informed
by a lively theology of marriage, the fruits of clerical/lay dialogue in CMAC work and training. By abandoning the schools
service, this body of experience in the CMAC, built up for fifteen
years or more, was lost to the educational system, as was the opportunity to build from the schools service, through pre-marriage and post-marriage courses, a continuum of pastoral support for marriage and family from one generation to the next.

Appendix 1: Relationships Education in Schools
(Belfast in the 1970s)

The following is an excerpt from *Education for Love,* a handbook for Christian sex education and education for personal relationships in secondary schools in the Diocese of Down and Connor, produced in the early 1970s by a committee appointed by Bishop Philbin to 'develop a broad programme of *Education for Love* which could be implemented in secondary schools':

'Sex in the narrower sense refers only to the reproductive organs and their function and the term sex education is often wrongly taken to mean instructing adolescents in this aspect alone. Real sex education sets out to prepare a boy for his role in life as a man and a girl for hers as a woman, and, in this sense, has always been implicitly part of the curriculum of the secondary school.' (Ch. 1, p. 6)

The copy below of a summary of a scheme for social studies (one of a number of such derived largely from pioneering EPR work in Catholic secondary schools in Belfast) is reproduced to give some sense of the scope of the subject, perceived in the terms of the quotation above:

Scheme for Northern Ireland CSE Social Studies. Mode 3 A Two Year Course
(circa late 1970s)

'The Family in Society' – An approach through the study of personal relationships

Aims:	1 To give some understanding of the establishment and maintenance of human relationships
	2 To show the importance of a sense of security as a basic necessity for healthy emotional growth at all ages
	3 To show the mutual dependence of the family and society.
The Course:	CHILDHOOD
	ADULTHOOD
Project work:	WOMEN TODAY
	STRESS IN MARRIAGE
	A CHILD GROWS UP
	WORKING WITH THE ELDERLY
	WORKING WITH THE HANDICAPPED
Assessment:	WRITTEN EXAMINATION
	COURSE WORK ASSESSMENT
	PROJECT WORK ASSESSMENT

Ninety subject headings for teachers are listed under the following subheads:

Childhood: Establishing the first relationships. Pregnancy and birth. Development of communication. The pre-school years. Deprivation.

Discipline. One-parent families. Widening circle of relationships. The child and the law. The generation gap. Adolescence. Transition from school to work.

Adulthood: The changing roles of men and women. Choosing a partner. Love. Marriage. Various rites of marriage. Alternative to marriage. Marriage conflict and breakdown. Family Planning. Housing and home making. Family leisure and recreation. Old age and its problems. Mental health in the community. Caring in the community. The future of the family.

Appendix 2: First Centres Foundation Years-1962-75

(The year of the first selection for the centre)

		Bishop	Centre Priest
1962	Belfast	+Daniel Mageean*	Fr Shaun McClafferty
1964	Cork	+Cornelius Lucey	Fr Frank Buckley
	Kilkenny	+Peter Birch	Fr Edward Wall
	Limerick	+Henry Murphy	Fr Michael Sadlier
1966	Newry	+Eugene O'Doherty	Fr Matt O'Hare
1967	Waterford	+Michael Russell	Fr Robert Arthur
	Wexford	+Donal Herlihy	Fr Matthew Berney
1968	Armagh#	Cardinal Conway	Fr John Bradley
	Dublin**	Archbishop McQuaid	Fr Michael Browne
1969	Carlow	+Patrick Lennon	Fr Lawrence Ryan
	Cloyne	+John Ahern	Fr Tom McSweeney
	Ennis	+Michael Harty	Fr Willie Walsh
	Cashel#	Archbishop Morris	Fr Andy Kennedy
	West Cork#	+Cornelius Lucey	Fr Donal Casey
1970	Drogheda	Cardinal Conway(A)	Fr James Crowley
		+John McCormack(M)	Fr James Bird
	Kerry#	+Eamon Casey	Fr Michael O'Doherty
	Nenagh#	+Michael Harty	Fr Eamon Gilmartin
1971	Castlebar	Archbishop Cunnane	Fr Tony King
	Galway	+Michael Browne	Fr Padraic O'Laoi
	Letterkenny#	+Anthony McFeely	Fr Owen Friel
	Tuam	Archbishop Cunnane	Fr Thomas Waldron
1972	Athlone	+Cahal Daly	Fr Colm O'Reilly
	Clogher#	+Patrick Mulligan	Fr Sean McNaboe
	Longford	+Cahal Daly	Fr Colm O'Reilly
	Newbridge	+Patrick Lennon	Fr Denis Harrington
	Sligo	+Dominic Conway	Fr D McLoughlin
1973	Cavan	+Francis J McKiernan	Fr P J McManus
	Derry	+Edward Daly	Fr Seamus O'Connell
	Dundalk	Cardinal Conway	Fr Sean McCartan
	Mullingar#	+John McCormack	Fr Eugene Conlon
1974	Omagh	+Edward Daly	Fr Colm O'Doherty
	Downpatrick	+William Philbin	Fr Joe Maguire
1975	Ballina	+Thomas McDonnell	Fr Patrick Gallagher

* Died before the centre opened. Succeeded by Bishop William Philbin.
**Dublin's first centre in Westland Row later moved to Harcourt St.
The next two, Marino and Dun Laoghaire, opened in 1975. By 1984
there were 9 centres in the Dublin diocese.
Centre subsequently sub-divided.

Appendix 3

National Chairman/Director/Chief Executive – Westminster

1946	Graham Graham-Green
1951	Fr Robert Gorman
1956	Fr Maurice O'Leary
1974	Fr Ben Chalmers
1976	Fr Peter Rudman
1982	Bernard Cawley
1987	Jean Judge
1993	Mary Corbett

National Director – Ireland

1975	Fr Andy Kennedy
1984	Fr Michael O'Doherty
1993	Fr Dan Cavanagh
1997	Liz Early (Temporary)
1998	Fr John Hannan

First Irish Tutor Body at 1971

Educational		*Counselling;*	
Sheila Campbell,	Belfast	Isobel Stewart,	Belfast
Brian Howlett	Dublin	Eithne Maguire,	Co Clare
Mary McKeogh,	Kilkenny	Chrissie Glancy,	Limerick
Tony Campbell,	Newry		
Jim Meehan,	Newry		

Additional tutors at 1973

Educational:	Beverly Carberry, Carlow
Counselling:	Darach Connolly, Dublin

Appendix 4: The Irish National Executive 1969-1975

(Elected at the Chairmen and Secretaries' meeting in Athlone in 1969)

Tony Campbell,	Newry
Fr Andy Kennedy,	Cashel
Paddy Maloney,	Dublin
Mary McKeogh,	Kilkenny

Their brief: to convene an Irish Annual Conference at Easter (The English Conferences were held in September) and to foster communication with centres, which would include issuing a Newsletter.

Other names which appeared later until it was superseded by the Executive Committee elected by the Assembly on 10 May 1975, were *(possibly not complete)*:

Fr Michael Browne	Dublin
Fr Frank Buckley	Cork (Replaced Fr Andy Kennedy in 1971)
Gavin Halpin	Drogheda
Jim Hewison	Waterford
Fr Willie Lee	Cashel (Priests)
Jim Meehan	Newry (Tutors)
Peter Nugent	Dublin (Replaced Mary McKeogh in 1974)
Elizabeth Roddy	Galway
Dr Maeve Twomey	Carlow (Doctors)

Chairmen in known order of succession:

Tony Campbell
Fr Andy Kennedy
Fr Frank Buckley
Fr Michael Browne

Irish Conferences 1970 –1975:

1970	Gormanston
1971	Gormanston
1972	Newbridge
1973	Galway
1974	Gormanston
1975	Clongowes

Appendix 5:
Delegates to the first Assembly 10 May 1975

Armagh	Seamus Quinn	Kerry	Fr Michael O'Doherty
Athlone	Mary Fitzpatrick	Kilkenny	Matt O'Brien
Belfast	Fr Hilary Armstrong*	Limerick	John Kernan
Carlow	Peter Fletcher	Longford	Gerry Hickey
Cashel	Fr Willie Lee	Monaghan	Kathleen McCaul
Cavan	Airmid O'Hanlon	Mullingar	Liam Murphy
Cloyne	Derry O'Driscoll	Nenagh	(See Ennis)
Cork	John McCarthy	Newbridge	Art Thornbury
Derry	William O'Donnell	Newry	Marie Toner
Downpatrick	Fr Fred McSorley*	Raphoe	Maurice Sweeney
Drogheda	Gavin Halpin	Sligo	Sean Burke
Dublin	Dr Jim Barnes	Tuam	Carmel Reynolds
Dundalk	Mary Deary	Waterford	Jim Hewison
Ennis	Eddie Fitzgerald	West Cork	Fr Donal Casey
Galway	Dr Moya O'Donnell	Wexford	Ann Small

(29 delegates listed. Note that Newsletter No 7 of June 1975 states '26 delegates representing 26 centres' – apparently in error.)

* The Belfast and Downpatrick delegates did not vote (not 'even once' according to the Newsletter) on the grounds that their centres (Down and Connor Marriage Advisory Service) 'formed an independent society associated with the CMAC'. Full integration to be considered in consultation with their bishop.

Elected by the Assembly (by ballot) on 10 May 1975
to serve on the National Executive Committee of CMAC Ireland

Dr Jim Barnes	(Dublin)
Jim Hewison	(Waterford)
John Kernan	(Limerick)
Fr Willie Lee	(Cashel)
Liam Murphy	(Mullingar)
Ann Small	(Wexford)

Appendix 6
Memorandum from Fr Michael Browne, Chairman INE, to the Episcopal Conference, May 1975

1. Historical
1.1 The Catholic Marriage Advisory Council (CMAC) is a relative newcomer on the Irish scene. The first centre was established in Belfast in 1963.
1.2 The pattern of establishment is much the same as in England and Scotland. A request from the bishop of the diocese has been followed by a meeting with Fr Maurice O'Leary, London, who arranged for the selection and training of counsellors.
1.3 There is a CMAC centre in nearly every diocese in Ireland; growth in the past few years has been rapid and there are now 30 centres in operation.
1.4 The local bishop appoints the Priest Director, and undertakes to finance the centre.

2. Personnel

2.1		
	Priests	120
	Counsellors	470
	Trainee Counsellors	118
	Doctors	95
	Nurses	153
	Legal Advisors	25
	TOTAL	981

2.2 In addition, a considerable number of married couples assist at Marriage Preparation Courses and Family Planning Sessions. These couples are not counsellors, although many of them attended selection conferences, but their contributions from practical experience of marriage are invaluable.

3. Constitutional Position
3.1 The CMAC in Ireland as such has no constitution.
3.2 It is now suggested that the Catholic Marriage Advisory Council, at present incorporated in England and Wales, should be incorporated as a *legal entity* in Ireland.
3.3 Such legal incorporation of CMAC here, would facilitate negotiation with Government Departments, Health Boards and other statutory bodies.
3.4 Historically, the present National Executive Committee of CMAC Ireland evolved from a small committee elected in 1969 at a meeting of Centre Chairmen and Secretaries held in Athlone.
3.5 Initially, the main function of the Executive Committee was to organise an Annual Conference for all the Irish Centres.

3.6 The Executive Committee as now constituted is empowered both by the Centres and the Hierarchy to negotiate financial aid both at central executive and local levels.

3.7 It is now agreed by the centres that we establish a new body, to be called THE ASSEMBLY of CMAC IRELAND which, subject to the Hierarchy, will be the general policy making and governing body of CMAC in this country.

3.8 Each centre will elect one member to represent it on the Assembly which will meet not less than once a year.

3.9 The Assembly will choose from amongst its members, an EXECU-TIVE COMMITTEE consisting of Chairman, Secretary, Treasurer and three other members. The Executive will have power to co-opt other members and appoint sub-committees.

3.10 The Hierarchy will be asked to appoint a National Priest Director who will also be an *ex-officio* member of the Assembly and the Executive Committee.

3.11 Such constitutional development of CMAC in Ireland seems appropriate at this time, because of

(a) the rapid growth in the number of centres and the need to 'service' them.

(b) the need to establish our National identity particularly vis-a-vis the Government for purposes of obtaining financial aid.

(c) The plain fact that London is unable any longer to cope with our requirements as well as their own.

4. Finance

4.1 CMAC is both conscious and appreciative of the fact that all the financial resources needed have been supplied to date by the Bishops.

4.2 While diocesan support will continue to be necessary and desirable, the National Executive Committee has applied to the Department of Health for subventions to local centres through Area Health Boards.

4.3 It is hoped that Bishops will continue as hitherto to support their centres so that subventions from the Health Boards can be used to cover increased costs and expansion.

4.4 Calculations and returns from Centres indicate that the annual sum needed for the average centre is £2,500. A few of the centres in the larger urban areas would need two or three times this amount.

4.5 The National Executive has also applied for a grant from central funds through the Department of Health to finance a national administrative office.

4.6 The application to the Department of Health (supra 4.2; 4.5) was discussed and agreed with the members of the Pastoral Commission of the Episcopal Conference. They were well received by the Minister, have since been the subject of consultation with his senior officials, and a favourable response is anticipated in the near future. How much? The present financial situation makes us less optimistic now than when the application was made twelve months ago.

4.7 The national administrative office is now essential for the purpose of consolidation and continuing growth – initially it will cost at least £10,000 per annum.

5. A Voluntary Service

5.1 CMAC provides remedial, educational and medical counselling through its personnel, all of whom contribute their services on an entirely voluntary basis and will continue to do so.

5.2 Nevertheless expenses inevitably arise for rent of premises, rates, electricity, telephone, stationery and postage. To preserve and enhance the quality of the service, it is very desirable that counsellors attend Conferences and In-service Training sessions, both at home and abroad, thus incurring travelling and subsistence expenses. Counsellors should where necessary be reimbursed also for out-of-pocket expenses, such as travelling long distances to the work assigned to them.

6. Relations with London

6.1 Fr Maurice O'Leary, who had been Priest Director of CMAC almost since its inception, departed from that office in November 1974. With his encouragement and assistance, and that of his successor, Fr Ben Chalmers, advantage was taken of the opportunity for a general re-assessment of CMAC as a service organisation.

6.2 The National Executive Committee of CMAC (Ireland) learned from Fr Chalmers at a specially convened meeting, that the Executive and Headquarters personnel in London could no longer provide the same standards of service to Irish Centres as in the past, partly due to the growth in numbers of centres already referred to and partly due to increased attention the British Centres called for by reassessment of the position over there.

6.3 It was agreed that the future aim would be independence with interdependence, the essential objectives being common high standards of selection and training, and constant striving for improved quality in all areas of counselling.

7. The Future

7.1 Arising from discussions with the London Executive, the National Executive of CMAC (Ireland) drew up proposals to facilitate a gradual and increasing assumption of responsibility for Selection Conferences, Basic Training, In-Service Training and supervision of the quality of counselling in Ireland.

7.2 In essence, these proposals are based on a national Assembly in which every Irish Centre will be represented and which will meet at least once a year. The Assembly will decide on policy matters, and will elect an Executive Committee to discharge agreed policy through a national administrative office.

7.3 The proposals were endorsed at the recent Annual Conference of CMAC (Ireland) and the first meeting of the new Assembly was called for Saturday, 10th May 1975 in Dublin.

8. National Priest Director

8.1 As an essential corollary to the developments outlined above, it was agreed at the Annual Conference that the Irish Hierarchy be requested to:

(a) appoint a full-time national Priest Director to CMAC (Ireland) who would be their representative on both the Assembly and the Executive Committee, and

(b) confirm their continuing financial support of local Centres and the national administrative office.

8.2 The need for a full-time Priest Director is urgent. CMAC is still too dependent on people coming from England to help with selection of counsellors and their training.

8.3 In the past two years the Dublin Centre has carried an unusually heavy burden of office and administrative work in respect of the CMAC in Ireland. At the same time Dublin's own needs continue to grow; it will have two new centres before the end of this year. All things considered, now would seem to be the appropriate time to appoint a National Director and set up a national office for CMAC. This step will ensure that the service here will have its own identity, and become more self-supporting. It may develop along somewhat different lines and there may be a different emphasis to that of the CMAC in England. It will, it is hoped, continue to provide an effective counselling service in the area of marriage and family life.

Michael Browne (signed)

Rev. Michael Browne,
Chairman,
National Executive (CMAC),
35 Harcourt Street,
Dublin 2

Bibliography

Papers:

'The CMAC Comes of Age', Graham J Graham-Green, CMAC Bulletin October 1986

'Marriage Preparation in the Catholic Church: Getting It Right', Centre For Marriage and Family, Creighton University, Omaha, Nebraska.

(Untitled) Canon Maurice O'Leary, Paper to CMAC Ireland annual conference, Clongowes, April 1988.

'Learning for Life', National Marriage Guidance Council, Rugby 1986.

Publications:

Marriage Care, John Marshall, Catholic Marriage Care Ltd, London 1996.

No Lions in the Hierarchy, Joseph Dunn, Columba Press , Dublin 1994.

No Vipers in the Vatican, Joseph Dunn, Columba Press, Dublin 1996.

A History of Ulster, Jonathan Bardon, Blackstaff Press, Belfast 1992.

Cardinal Bernard Griffin, Archbishop of Westminster, Michael de la Bedoyere, Rocklif Corporation, London 1995.

Ireland Since the Famine, FSL Lyons, Fontana, London 1990.

Humanae Vitae, Pope Paul VI, trs Alan C Clark, CTS, London 1968.

Familiaris Consortio: Christian Family in the Modern World, CTS, London 1981.

Jack Dominian, Jock Dalrymple, Geoffrey Chapman, London 1995.

Marriage Matters, Home Office Report (Britain) 1979.

Client-Centred Therapy, Carl R Rogers, Constable & Co Ltd, London 1951.

On Becoming a Person, Carl R Rogers, Constable & Co Ltd, London 1961.

God, Where are You? Gerard W Hughes, Darton, Longman & Todd Ltd, London 1997.

Relationship: The Heart of Helping People, Helen Harris Perlman, University of Chicago University Press 1979.

The Skilled Helper, Gerard Egan, Brooks/Cole Publishing Co, a division of International Thompson Publishing Inc. Fourth edition 1990.

Who Should Care? The Development of Kilkenny Social Services 1963-1980, Sr Stanislaus Kennedy RSC, Turoe Press, Dublin 1981.

Notes

PREFACE
1. See Bibliography

INTRODUCTION
1. *Jack Dominian: Lay Prophet?*, J. Dalrymple, p 133
2. Marriage Matters, Home Office Report (Britain), 1980, HMSO, p 14

CHAPTER 1: GENESIS
1. Quotations, unless otherwise stated, from 'The CMAC Comes of Age' by Graham-Green, published in the CMAC Bulletin, October 1986.
2. From the minutes of the first meeting of the CMAC Advisory Committee, 26 February 1946. The last sentence in the reproduction on p. 18 ends: 'and the Chairman reported in reply to a question that there would be no objection to such title from Dr Mace.'
3. Eirene Graham-Green in correspondence with the author in 1996.
4. From a copy of the address supplied by Veronica Graham-Green December 1996.

CHAPTER 2: CARDINAL GRIFFIN
1. 'The Archbishop of Westminster', The Right Rev George A Beck, AA. Bishop of Salford. From the *Westminster Cathedral Chronicle*, November 1956 (special edition). (WCC)
2. Correspondence with the author, 1996.
3. Interview with the author, May 1996.
4. From 'Out of the Catacombs', Cardinal Griffin, WCC.
5. Ibid. In this address the Cardinal reminded his audience that since the restoration of the hierarchy in 1850 (which at the time aroused an outbreak of anti-papist agitation), the Catholic population in England had increased from one million to three millions and Catholics were now accepted as an integral part of the nation. Catholics, he claimed, were well represented in positions of influence, in the universities, the professions and in the services. Being loyal to their church strengthened rather than diminished their loyalty to the crown. 'It is now taken for granted that as Catholics our loyalty to the throne is in no sense diminished.'
6. 'A Spiritual Legacy', The Right Rev Mgr Derek Warlock, WCC.

CHAPTER 3: FR GORMAN

1. Fr Gorman stopped the practice of having case-notes typed up and successfully resisted a Home Office proposal to have case-notes open to their inspectors.

CHAPTER 4: CANON O'LEARY

1. This and other quotations from interviews with the author, 1996, unless otherwise stated.
2. Paper to the Irish CMAC Conference at Clongowes, April 1988.
3. Ibid
4. *Jack Dominian: Lay Prophet?*, Dalrymple, pp 37-38.
5. Paper to the Irish Conference at Clongowes 1988.
6. Ibid.
7. Ibid.
8. Letter to counsellors from Fr O'Leary, 20 July 1968.
9. Address to CMAC Conference, Keele University, 27-29 September, 1968.
10. Correspondence with author, 1996.
11. Correspondence with author, 1996.
12. 'Reflections on CMAC (Ireland)', Nicholas Tyndall, herein.
13. Correspondence with the author, 1997.

CHAPTER 5: EARLY YEARS

1. Full title: 'The Pontifical Commission for the Study of Population, the Family and Birth'.
2. From interviews or correspondence with the author in 1996 unless otherwise stated.
3. *Jack Dominian: Lay Prophet?*, Jock Dalrymple, p 64. See Bibliography.
4. See above publication for a full list of Dominian's publications.
5. Ibid., p 133.
6. Ibid., p 97.

CHAPTER 6: THE IRISH CONNECTION THROUGH ENGLISH EYES

1. The first centre was in Westland Row for two years.
2. Fr Kennedy was sent, not by the Irish bishops, but by his own bishop, Archbishop Morris.
3. Actually 35 centres

CHAPTER 7: TWO CULTURES – ONE FAITH

1. All quotations from correspondence with the author, 1996.

CHAPTER 8: THE ROLE OF THE DOCTORS

1. The doctors in Dublin mentioned by Canon O'Leary are Dr Joe Barnes and Dr Ivor Drury. Belfast doctors associated with Dr Magill were Dr J P Donaghy and Dr Sean Gibson. There were of course many other doctors in support in both centres.

2. Paper given to the Irish CMAC Conference, Clongowes, April 1988.

3. Marshall in interview with the author, April 1996. See also *Marriage Care*, p 101.

4. All quotations from Dr Magill are from interviews with the author in 1996.

CHAPTER 9: THE BIRTH OF THE BELFAST CENTRE

1. Paper to the Irish CMAC Conference, Clongowes, April 1988.

2. Ibid.

3. Gerard Benedict Newe M.A., D.Litt. Born Cushendall 1907, died 1982. Secretary to the NI Council of Social Services 1948-1972. Made history as the only Catholic to serve as Minister in the old Stormont Government at the invitation of the PM, Brian Faulkner, in the interest of better community relations. He served in government from October 1971 until the dissolution in March 1972.

4. In the early years the Belfast centre received funding from the Stormont government on the basis that it was a service centre for the North, (similar to the Belfast office of the NMGC). It has been said that Cardinal Conway, then Archbishop in Armagh, intervened successfully to obtain a grant for the centre from central government but searches in Ard Coeli and PRONI failed to uncover any evidence of this. Belfast centre assisted in the basic training of the Newry centre in 1966/7. About 1975/6 the central government grant to the Belfast centre was replaced by an annual grant from the local Health Board.

5. Recorded by Fr McClafferty as 'Mary F McNally'.

6. Fr McClafferty's diary.

7. Ibid.

8. At the meeting of the first Assembly in Dublin in May 1975 the Down and Connor centres' representatives, Fr Hilary Armstrong and Fr Fred McSorley, refrained from voting on the grounds that their centres were not part of the CMAC.

CHAPTER 10: FROM DUBLIN TO BELFAST AND BEYOND

1. See Appendix for list of first centres in chronological order.

2. Cork centre was closed by Bishop Lucey for a time in 1972, when the counsellors refused to accept that a doctor had breached confidentiality by quoting in a public address the percentage of people seeking help for family planning. (M 74)

3. Correspondence from David S Sheehy , Dublin Diocesan Archives, to Peter Nugent 1996.

4. Communication from Peter Nugent.

5. Ibid.

6. Mary McKeogh in correspondence with the author, 1996.

7. *Who Should Care – The Development of Kilkenny Social Services 1963-1980*, p 70.

8. Kilkenny centre, having effectively lost the support of the bishop,

lapsed and was closed down as a CMAC centre in 1977. It was replaced as the Ossory Marriage Advisory Service under Fr Dan Cavanagh (later National Director of Accord) and returned to the CMAC fold in 1982.

CHAPTER 11: INDEPENDENCE
1. See appendix for full transcript.

CHAPTER 12: THE IRISH NATIONAL EXECUTIVE
1. These six had the distinction of being among the first group of tutors to be trained in Ireland (in Bellinter 1976).

CHAPTER 13: THE GOVERNMENT GRANT
1. From minutes of a meeting of the Pastoral Commission, Limerick, 1 September 1977: 'Specific figures were available which had been given to centres by Regional Health Boards and in 1976 this figure totalled about £2,000.'

CHAPTER 14: TOWARDS A NEW CONSTITUTION
1. The working party consisted of Dr (now Bishop) Larry Ryan; Darach Connolly, legal advisor; and Seamus Flanagan from Limerick. Also involved in negotiations were Peter Sefton and Philip Leonard as Northern Ireland representatives.
2. Bishop McCormack to Fr Kennedy, letter dated 25 November 1980.

CHAPTER 15: THE CENTRAL OFFICE
1. These were the conditions up to circa 1984. Things may have changed substantially by the time this is published.
2. We will see later how Fr Kennedy met this situation with his brilliantly conceived 'tutor-per-centre' scheme.

CHAPTER 16: THE KENNEDY YEARS
1. Not by the Irish bishops, as incorrectly stated by Marshall (M 36 & 74).
2. 465,672 according to the CMAC Progress Report 1984.
3. The constitution is not signed by representatives of either the bishops or the NEC and has no date of coming into effect. These, and the 'three year' provision, are contained in a letter from Bishop McCormack to Fr Kennedy of 25 November 1980. The constitution, with some minor amendments, including the change of name to 'Accord', is still in force at time of writing.
4. It is possible that the idea was a product of a 'Think Tank' set up by Fr Kennedy in 1978. Unfortunately no record of this body can be uncovered.

CHAPTER 17: THE BISHOPS AND THE CMAC
1. *No Vipers in the Vatican*, p 299.

CHAPTER 19: MARRIAGE COUNSELLING IN THE CMAC

1. In his *On Becoming a Person*, Rogers gives a touching account of a turning point towards client-centred counselling when the mother of one of his child clients, almost as an after-thought, departed from her 'sterile case history' regarding her child to pour out her own troubles in her marriage. 'Real therapy began then.' (p 11).

2. *Client -Centred Therapy*, p 21.

3. Paper to the Irish CMAC Conference, Clongowes, April 1988.

4. *God Where Are You?* Gerard W Hughes, Darton Longman & Todd, London 1997, pp 124-5.

5. Fr McClafferty's diary, entry 30 September 1962.

6. *The Casework Relationship*, Loyola University Press 1957, and George Allen & Unwin London 1961, Foreword.

7. *Client Centred Therapy*, p 27.

8. Ibid., p 22.

9. Ibid., pp 25-6.

10. See Carkhuff's *Helping and Human Relationships*, 1969.

11. *The Skilled Helper*, Fourth Edition, p. 8.

12. From *Supervision in the Helping Professions*, Hawkins and Shohet, OUP 1989.

13. *The Skilled Helper*, Fourth Edition, p 8.

CHAPTER 20: THE PRE-MARRIAGE COURSES

1. *Pre-Nuptial Enquiry. Pastoral Guidelines*, Irish Episcopal Conference 1991.

2. *Familiaris Consortio*, n 66.

3. *Marriage Preparation In The Catholic Church – Getting It Right*, Centre for Marriage and Family, Creighton University, Omaha, Nebraska, 68178. USA, Nov 1995.

4. 'The CMAC Comes of Age', Graham J Graham-Green, *Bulletin of the CMAC*, London, October 1986.

5. Ibid.

6. 'Marriage Education', Sue Waldron-Skinner in the *Bulletin of Marriage Enrichment*, London.

7. As for footnote 3.

8. It is extraordinary how this fact escapes many who are unfamiliar with the work. It is not uncommon for priests (and occasionally a bishop) to enquire if candidates *not* selected as counsellors could be employed to deliver the pre-marriage courses!

9. The Campbell couple found it better to work together because their counsellor colleagues found it difficult to accept the idea of 'minimum input'!

10. 'Marriage Preparation – Making Better Lovers', Brian Howlett. Paper to NMGC study day 1986, published in *Learning for Life*, p 15 (See bibliography).

11. Raymond McCourt, another Newry counsellor, promoted this

method, translating the exercises from American to a more acceptable Irish idiom.

12. *Learning for Life*, p 12.

13. One couple described how a speaker 'placed his backside on the table and regaled us for an hour to a most entertaining discourse. We enjoyed it immensely.'!

14. One centre invited two trainee counsellors to attend a course as observers. Their surprising discovery was that the bonding which had been so carefully built up was impaired by the introduction of visual aids and by some role play by the counsellors.

15. *The Creighton Report*. See Footnote 3.

16. Sue Waldron-Skinner. See Footnote 6.

17. Family Caring Trust, Newsletter No 29, April 1996.

CHAPTER 21: THE NFP SERVICE

1. See 'The Role of the Doctors' herein.

2. *Casti Connubii*, Pope Pius X1 (1930), *Hunanae Vitae*, Pope Paul VI (1968) and others.

3. Addendum to *The Holy Family Bible*, Harwin Press (in conjunction with The Catholic Press INC) Virtue and Co London 1961.

4. Marie Stopes was born in Edinburgh, 15 October 1880. A botanist, she specialised in fossil plants and the origins of coal. Her PhD in 1904 was one of the first awarded in botany to a woman. She taught in Manchester University and was married again to H V Roe, an aircraft manufacturer who supported her in her birth control campaign. She died in Surrey on 2 October 1958.

5. See 'The Role of the Doctors' herein.

6. The term 'symptothermic' is now used to include other identifiable body symptoms in addition to changes in the cervical mucus.

7. Professor Bonnar of UCD was a leading promoter of natural methods of birth control, as was Dr Anna Flynn, an Irish obstetrician working in Birmingham.

8. WHO, a specialised agency of the United Nations established in 1948.

9. The IFFLP folded as an international organisation in 1997. It still exists at zonal level – each continent being a zone.

10. It is not clear at what point the CMAC took over from the WHO to pay Mary Higgins' salary.

CHAPTER 22: THE CMAC SCHOOLS SERVICE

1. Vat II, *Declaration on Christian Education*.

2. CMAC Newsletter No 5, February 1975.

3. In the recollection of one Belfast counsellor, the reason given by Fr McClafferty was that he did not have the time to supervise it.

4. In the South in the 1940s and 50s the banning of books with the slightest reference to sexuality reflected the prevailing negative attitude to the subject, e.g. Dr Halliday Sutherland's *Laws of Life*, which explained

the woman's menstrual cycle, was banned even though it had the imprimatur of the English Catholic bishops.

5. CMAC booklet, *Education Counselling*, circa 1978.

6. Rogers claimed that student-centred education produced people educated to be 'rulers', the basis of democracy, whereas the traditional education produces 'well informed technicians who will be completely amenable to carrying out all orders of constituted authority without question'. *Client Centred Therapy*, p 387.

7. In Granard, Co Longford, a young girl gave birth to a baby in a grotto. Both were found dead the following morning,

8. Quotations from a Family Solidarity pamphlet issued August 1985.